FAMILY
COOKING
IN ~ COLOUR

FAMILY
COOKING
IN ~ COLOUR

DELICIOUS, INNOVATIVE RECIPES, STEP-BY-STEP

LAURA WASHBURN

AND

CARLA CAPALBO

ULTIMATE
EDITIONS

First published in 1995 by Ultimate Editions

© Anness Publishing Limited 1995

Ultimate Editions is an imprint of
Anness Publishing Limited
Boundary Row Studios
1 Boundary Row
London SE1 8HP

Distributed in Australia by Reed Editions

This edition distributed in Canada by Book Express
an imprint of Raincoast Books Distribution Limited

ISBN 1 86035 006 2

Editorial Director: Joanna Lorenz
Series Editor: Linda Fraser
Photographer: Amanda Heywood
Food for Photography: Elizabeth Wolf Cohen

Typeset by MC Typeset Limited
Printed and bound in Singapore

MEASUREMENTS
Three sets of equivalent measurements have been provided in the recipes here, in
the following order: Metric, Imperial and American. It is essential that units of
measurements are not mixed within each recipe.

Contents

SOUPS

Warming soups make a welcoming start to a meal at any time of the year, and whether you are cooking for family meals or a special dinner party there are plenty of recipes here to choose from: chunky fish chowders; a traditional Pea and Ham Broth, which would make a filling lunch-time meal served with crusty bread or crisp toasted croûtes; delicious vegetable and lentil soups; and an innovative, equally tasty soup flavoured with blueberries. Soups are often only served on cooler days, yet included here are two chilled soups to make when the weather is warm; a delicate creamy avocado soup perfect for summer evening dinner parties, and a slightly spicy Gazpacho which would make a delicious beginning to a lunch in the garden or even a picnic.

PRAWN AND SWEETCORN CHOWDER

Serves 4

30ml/2 tbsp olive oil
1 onion, finely chopped
50g/2oz/4 tbsp butter or margarine
25g/1oz/¼ cup plain flour
750ml/1¼ pints/3 cups fish or chicken
    stock, or clam juice
250ml/8fl oz/1 cup milk
225g/8oz cooked, peeled prawns
350g/12oz sweetcorn (fresh, frozen
    or canned)
2.5ml/½ tsp finely chopped fresh dill
    or thyme
Tabasco sauce
120ml/4fl oz/½ cup single cream
salt
fresh dill sprigs, to garnish

1 Heat the olive oil in a large heavy-based saucepan. Add the onion to the pan and cook over a low heat for 8–10 minutes, until softened.

2 Meanwhile, melt the butter or margarine in a separate saucepan. Add the flour and stir until thoroughly blended. Cook over a low heat for 1–2 minutes, then pour in the stock and milk and stir to blend. Bring to the boil over a medium heat and cook for 5–8 minutes, stirring frequently.

3 Chop the prawns and add to the onion with the sweetcorn and chopped fresh dill or thyme. Cook for 2–3 minutes over a low heat, stirring occasionally, then set aside.

4 Add the sauce to the prawn and sweetcorn mixture and mix well. Remove 600ml/1 pint/2½ cups of the soup and purée in a blender or food processor. Stir into the rest of the soup in the pan. Season with salt and add Tabasco sauce to taste.

5 Add the cream and stir to blend. Heat the soup almost to boiling point, stirring frequently. Serve hot garnished with dill sprigs.

SALMON CHOWDER

INGREDIENTS

Serves 4

25g/1oz/2 tbsp butter or margarine
1 onion, finely chopped
1 leek, finely chopped
fennel bulb, finely chopped
30ml/2 tbsp plain flour
1.2 litres/2 pints/5 cups fish stock
2 medium-size potatoes, cut into
    1cm/½in cubes
450g/1lb boneless, skinless salmon, cut
    into 2cm/¾in cubes
175ml/6fl oz/¾ cup milk
120ml/4fl oz/½ cup single cream
salt and black pepper
30ml/2 tbsp chopped fresh dill

1 Melt the butter or margarine in a large saucepan. Add the onion, leek and fennel and cook over a medium heat for 5–8 minutes, until softened, stirring occasionally.

2 Stir in the flour. Reduce the heat to low and cook, stirring occasionally, for a further 3 minutes.

3 Add the stock and potatoes and season with salt and pepper. Bring to a boil, then reduce the heat, cover, and simmer for about 20 minutes, until the potatoes are tender.

4 Add the salmon cubes and simmer for 3–5 minutes, until just cooked.

5 Stir in the milk, cream and dill and cook until just warmed through; do not boil. Taste and adjust the seasoning, if necessary, then serve.

TURKEY AND LENTIL SOUP

INGREDIENTS

Serves 4

25g/1oz/2 tbsp butter or margarine
1 large carrot, chopped
1 onion, chopped
1 leek, white part only, chopped
1 celery stalk, chopped
115g/4oz mushrooms, chopped
45ml/3 tbsp dry white wine
1 litre/1¾ pints/4 cups chicken stock
10ml/2 tsp dried thyme
1 bay leaf
115g/4oz/½ cup brown or green lentils
225g/8oz cooked turkey, diced
salt and black pepper

1 Melt the butter or margarine in a large saucepan. Add the carrot, onion, leek, celery and mushrooms. Cook for 3–5 minutes, until softened.

3 Add the lentils and continue cooking, covered, for 30–40 minutes more, until they are just tender. Stir the soup from time to time.

2 Stir in the wine and chicken stock. Bring to the boil and skim off any foam that rises to the surface. Add the thyme and bay leaf. Reduce the heat, cover, and simmer for 30 minutes.

4 Stir in the diced turkey and season to taste with salt and pepper. Cook until just heated through. Ladle the soup into bowls and serve hot.

TOMATO AND BLUE CHEESE SOUP

Serves 4

1.5kg/3lb ripe tomatoes, peeled, quartered, and seeded
2 garlic cloves, finely chopped
30ml/2 tbsp vegetable oil
1 leek, chopped
1 carrot, chopped
1 litre/1³/₄ pints/4 cups unsalted chicken stock
115g/4oz blue cheese, cut into smallish pieces
45ml/3 tbsp single cream
a few fresh basil leaves, plus extra for garnishing
175g/6oz bacon, cooked and crumbled
salt and black pepper

1 Preheat the oven to 200°C/400°F/ Gas 6. Spread the tomatoes in a shallow baking dish with the garlic.

2 Add seasoning to taste and bake for about 35 minutes.

3 Heat the oil in a large saucepan. Add the leek and carrot and season lightly with salt and pepper. Cook over a low heat for 10 minutes, stirring occasionally, until softened.

4 Stir in the stock and tomatoes. Bring to the boil, then lower the heat, cover and simmer for 20 minutes.

5 Add the blue cheese, cream and basil. Transfer to a food processor or blender and process until smooth, working in batches if necessary. Taste and adjust the seasoning.

6 Reheat the soup, but do not boil. Ladle into bowls and garnish with the crumbled bacon and basil.

PEA AND HAM BROTH

Serves 8

450g/1lb/2½ cups dried green or yellow split peas
1.85 litres/3¼ pints/8 cups water
1 ham bone with some meat left on it, or 1 ham hock
1 onion, finely chopped
1 leek, sliced
2 celery sticks, finely sliced
a few fresh parsley sprigs
6 black peppercorns
2 bay leaves
salt
flat leaf parsley, to garnish

1 Rinse the split peas under cold running water. Place the peas in a large pan and add water to cover. Bring to the boil and boil for 2 minutes. Remove the pan from the heat and leave to soak for 1 hour. Drain.

2 Return the peas to the pan and add the measured water, ham bone or hock, onion, leeks, celery, a couple of sprigs of parsley, salt, peppercorns and bay leaves. Bring to the boil, then reduce the heat, cover and simmer gently for 1–1½ hours, until the peas are tender. Skim occasionally.

3 Remove the bay leaves and the ham bone or hock from the soup. Cut the meat off the bone, discarding any fat and chop the meat into small cubes. Set the meat aside. Discard the ham bone and the bay leaves.

4 Purée the soup in batches in a food processor or blender. Pour into a clean saucepan and add the chopped ham. Check the seasoning. Simmer the soup for 3–4 minutes to heat through before serving. Garnish with parsley.

CREAMY PUMPKIN SOUP

INGREDIENTS

Serves 6
45ml/3 tbsp olive oil
½ onion, sliced
6 spring onions, white and green parts
*   sliced separately*
large pinch of cayenne pepper
1.25ml/¼ tsp ground cumin
large pinch of ground nutmeg
*   or mace*
600ml/1 pint/2½ cups pumpkin purée
1.2 litres/2 pints/5 cups chicken stock
2.5ml/½ tsp salt
250ml/8fl oz/1 cup single cream

1 Heat the oil in a large heavy-based saucepan. Add the onion and white spring onion and cook over a low heat for 8–10 minutes, until softened.

2 Add the spices, stir well and cook for 3–4 minutes. Add the pumpkin purée, stock and salt. Increase the heat slightly and cook for 15 minutes, stirring occasionally.

3 Leave the soup to cool, then purée in a food processor or blender.

4 Return the soup to the pan. Taste and add more cayenne pepper and salt if desired. Heat until the soup is just simmering. Stir in most of the cream and simmer for 2–3 minutes more. Serve hot, with a swirl of cream and the sliced green spring onions.

BEEF AND BLUEBERRY SOUP

INGREDIENTS

Serves 4
30ml/2 tbsp vegetable oil
450g/1lb sirloin steaks
175g/6oz/1½ cups finely sliced onions
25g/1oz/2 tbsp butter
1 litre/1¾ pints/4 cups beef stock
2.5ml/½ tsp salt
150g/5oz/1 cup blueberries or
*   blackcurrants, lightly mashed*
15ml/1 tbsp clear honey

2 Reduce the heat to low and add the onions and butter to the pan. Stir well, scraping up the meat juices. Cook over a low heat for 8–10 minutes, until the onions are softened.

4 Meanwhile, cut the steaks into thin strips using a sharp knife.

5 Taste the soup and add more salt or honey if necessary. Add the steak and its juices to the pan. Stir and cook for 30 seconds, then serve at once.

1 Heat the oil in a heavy saucepan until almost smoking. Add the steaks and brown on both sides over a medium-high heat. Remove the steaks from the pan and set aside.

3 Add the stock and salt and bring to the boil, stirring well. Mix in the blueberries or blackcurrants and honey. Simmer for 20 minutes.

CHILLED AVOCADO SOUP

Serves 4

2 large or 3 medium ripe avocados
15ml/1 tbsp fresh lemon juice
¼ cucumber, peeled and coarsely
  chopped
30ml/2 tbsp dry sherry
4 spring onions, roughly chopped
475ml/16fl oz/2 cups chicken stock
a few drops of Tabasco sauce (optional)
salt
natural yogurt or soured cream,
  to serve

1 Halve the avocados, remove the stones, and peel. Roughly chop the flesh and place in a food processor or blender. Add the lemon juice and process until very smooth.

2 Add the cucumber, sherry and most of the chopped spring onions. Process again until very smooth.

3 Transfer the avocado mixture to a large bowl, add the chicken stock and whisk until well blended. Season the soup with salt to taste and Tabasco sauce, if desired. Cover the bowl with clear film and chill well.

4 To serve, pour the soup into individual bowls. Swirl a spoonful of yogurt or soured cream in the centre of each bowl. Sprinkle with the reserved spring onions.

GAZPACHO

Serves 4

½ cucumber (about 225g/8oz), coarsely chopped
½ green pepper, seeded and coarsely chopped
½ red pepper, seeded and coarsely chopped
1 large tomato, coarsely chopped
2 spring onions, chopped
Tabasco sauce (optional)
45ml/3 tbsp chopped fresh parsley or coriander, to garnish
croûtons, to serve

For the soup base

450g/1lb ripe tomatoes, peeled, seeded and chopped
15ml/1 tbsp tomato ketchup
30ml/2 tbsp tomato purée
1.25ml/¼ tsp sugar
3.75ml/¾ tsp salt
1 tsp black pepper
45ml/3 tbsp sherry vinegar
175ml/6fl oz/¾ cup olive oil
350ml/12fl oz/1½ cups tomato juice

2 Add the ketchup, tomato purée, sugar, salt, pepper, vinegar and oil and pulse on and off 3–4 times, just to blend. Transfer to a large bowl and stir in the tomato juice.

3 Place the cucumber and green and red peppers in the food processor or blender and pulse on and off until finely chopped; do not overmix.

4 Reserve about 30ml/2 tbsp of the chopped vegetables for garnishing; stir the remainder into the soup. Taste for seasoning. Mix in the chopped tomato, spring onions and a dash of Tabasco sauce, if desired. Chill well.

5 To serve, ladle into bowls and sprinkle with the reserved chopped vegetables, chopped fresh parsley or coriander and the croûtons.

1 First make the soup base. Put the tomatoes in a food processor or blender and pulse on and off until just smooth, scraping the sides of the container occasionally.

Starters and Snacks

There's a delicious variety of starters and snacks to choose from here. You'll find a selection of light summery salads; a colourful and flavour-packed Mexican Mixed Salad which could be served at any time of the year; fish and seafood dishes for every occasion; a chilli-flavoured dip to serve with crudités; and nutty, stuffed eggs and celery sticks for a summer buffet. Many of the dishes can be prepared ahead, which is a boon if you are entertaining, and others are so quick and easy that they can be made in next to no time. If you are looking for a light snack there are two with a Mediterranean flavour: Turkey and Avocado Pitta Pizzas, and Toasted Tomato Sandwiches. If you have plenty of time to cook, Beetroot and Corned Beef Hash makes both delicious and filling fare throughout the year.

SCALLOP AND MUSSEL KEBABS

INGREDIENTS

Serves 4

65g/2½oz/5 tbsp butter, at room
   temperature
30ml/2 tbsp finely chopped fresh fennel
   fronds or parsley
15ml/1 tbsp fresh lemon juice
32 small scallops
24 large mussels in the shell
8 bacon rashers
115g/4oz/1 cup fresh white
   breadcrumbs
45ml/3 tbsp olive oil
salt and black pepper
parsley sprigs and lemon peel,
   to garnish
hot toast, to serve

1 Make the flavoured butter by combining the butter with the chopped herbs, lemon juice and salt and pepper to taste. Mix well. Set aside.

2 In a small saucepan, cook the scallops in their own liquid for about 5 minutes, or until just tender. (If there is no scallop liquid – retained from the shells after shucking – use a little fish stock or white wine.) Drain and pat dry with kitchen paper.

3 Scrub the mussels well, discarding any broken ones, and rinse under cold running water. Place in a large saucepan with about 2.5cm/1in of water. Cover the pan and steam the mussels over a medium heat until they open. Remove them from their shells, and pat dry on kitchen paper. Discard any mussels that have not opened.

4 Thread four scallops, three mussels and a rasher of bacon on to eight 15cm/6in wooden or metal skewers, weaving the bacon between the scallops and mussels.

5 Preheat the grill. Spread out the breadcrumbs on a plate. Brush the seafood with olive oil and roll in the crumbs to coat all over.

6 Place the skewers on the grill rack. Grill for 4–5 minutes on each side until crisp and lightly browned. Serve immediately garnished with the parsley sprigs and lemon peel and accompanied by hot toast and the flavoured butter.

MELON AND CRAB SALAD

Serves 6
450g/1lb fresh crab meat
120ml/4fl oz/½ cup mayonnaise
45ml/3 tbsp soured cream or
 natural yogurt
30ml/2 tbsp olive oil
30ml/2 tbsp fresh lemon or
 lime juice
2–3 spring onions, finely chopped
30ml/2 tbsp finely chopped fresh
 coriander
1.25ml/¼ tsp cayenne pepper
salt and black pepper
1½ canteloupe or small honeydew
 melons
3 medium chicory heads
fresh coriander sprigs, to garnish

1 Pick over the crab meat very carefully, removing any bits of shell or cartilage. Leave the pieces of crab meat as large as possible.

2 In a medium-sized bowl, combine all the other ingredients except the melons and chicory, and mix well. Fold the crab meat into this dressing.

3 Halve the melons and remove and discard the seeds. Cut them into thin slices, then remove the rind.

4 Arrange the salad on six individual serving plates, making a decorative design with the melon slices and whole chicory leaves. Place a mound of dressed crab meat on each plate and garnish the salads with one or two fresh coriander sprigs.

MUSSELS WITH CREAM AND PARSLEY

Serves 2
675g/1¹/₂lb mussels in the shell
¹/₂ fennel bulb, finely chopped
1 shallot, finely chopped
45ml/3 tbsp dry white wine
45ml/3 tbsp single cream
30ml/2 tbsp chopped fresh parsley
freshly ground black pepper

1 Scrub the mussels under cold running water. Remove any barnacles with a small knife and tear away the beards. Rinse once more.

2 Place the mussels in a large wide pan with a lid. Sprinkle them with the fennel, shallot and wine. Cover and place over a medium-high heat shaking the pan occasionally. Steam for 3–5 minutes, until the mussels open.

3 Lift out the mussels with a slotted spoon and remove the top shells. Discard any that did not open. Arrange the mussels, on their bottom shells, in one layer in a shallow serving dish. Cover and keep warm in a low oven.

4 Place a double layer of dampened muslin or a clean tea towel in a sieve set over a bowl. Strain the mussel cooking liquid through the muslin or tea towel. Return the liquid to a clean saucepan and bring to the boil.

5 Add the cream, stir well and boil for 3 minutes to reduce slightly, then stir in the parsley. Spoon the sauce over the mussels and sprinkle with freshly ground black pepper. Serve the mussels immediately.

AVOCADO AND PAW PAW SALAD

Serves 4

2 ripe avocados
1 ripe paw paw
1 large orange
1 small red onion
25–50g/1–2oz small rocket leaves or
   lamb's lettuce

For the dressing
60ml/4 tbsp olive oil
30ml/2 tbsp fresh lemon or lime juice
salt and black pepper

1 Halve the avocados and remove the stones. Carefully peel off the skin, then cut each avocado half lengthways into thick slices.

2 Peel the paw paw. Cut it in half lengthways and scoop out the seeds with a spoon. Set aside 15ml/1 tsp of the seeds for the dressing. Cut each paw paw half lengthways into eight slices.

3 Peel the orange. Using a small sharp knife, cut out the segments, cutting either side of the dividing membranes. Cut the onion into very thin slices and separate into rings.

4 Combine the dressing ingredients in a small bowl and mix well. Stir in the reserved paw paw seeds.

5 Assemble the salad on four individual serving plates. Alternate slices of paw paw and avocado. Add the orange segments and a small mound of rocket topped with onion rings. Spoon over the dressing.

ASPARAGUS WITH CREAMY VINAIGRETTE

INGREDIENTS

Serves 4

675g/1½lb asparagus spears
30ml/2 tbsp raspberry vinegar
2.5ml/½ tsp salt
5ml/1 tsp Dijon mustard
75ml/5 tbsp sunflower oil
30ml/2 tbsp soured cream or
   natural yogurt
white pepper
175g/6oz fresh raspberries

1 Fill a large shallow saucepan with water – it needs to be about 10cm/4in deep. Bring to the boil.

2 Trim off the tough ends from the asparagus spears. You may need to remove 2.5–5cm/1–2in from each spear.

3 Tie the asparagus spears into two bundles. Lower the bundles into the boiling water and cook for 5–7 minutes, until just tender.

4 Carefully remove the asparagus bundles from the boiling water and immediately immerse them in cold water to prevent further cooking. Drain and untie the bundles. Pat dry the spears with kitchen paper. Chill the asparagus for at least 1 hour.

5 Place the vinegar and salt in a bowl and stir with a fork until the salt is dissolved. Stir in the mustard, then gradually whisk in the oil until blended. Add the soured cream or yogurt and pepper to taste.

6 To serve, arrange the asparagus spears on individual plates and drizzle the dressing across the middle of the spears. Garnish with the fresh raspberries and serve at once.

EGG AND TOMATO SALAD WITH CRAB

──── INGREDIENTS ────

Serves 4
1 round lettuce
2 × 200g/7oz cans crab meat, drained
4 hard-boiled eggs, sliced
16 cherry tomatoes, halved
½ green pepper, seeded and
    thinly sliced
6 stoned black olives, sliced

For the dressing
250ml/8fl oz/1 cup mayonnaise
10ml/2 tsp fresh lemon juice
45ml/3 tbsp chilli sauce
½ green pepper, seeded and finely
    chopped
5ml/1 tsp horseradish sauce
5ml/1 tsp Worcestershire sauce

1 To make the dressing, place all the ingredients in a bowl and mix well. Set aside in a cool place.

2 Line four plates with the lettuce leaves. Mound the crab meat in the centre. Arrange the eggs around the outside with the tomatoes on top.

3 Spoon some of the dressing over the crab meat. Arrange the green pepper slices on top and sprinkle with the olives. Serve immediately with the remaining dressing.

SUMMER TUNA SALAD

──── INGREDIENTS ────

Serves 4–6
175g/6oz radishes
1 cucumber
3 celery sticks
1 yellow pepper
175g/6oz cherry tomatoes, halved
4 spring onions, thinly sliced
45ml/3 tbsp fresh lemon juice
45ml/3 tbsp olive oil
2 × 200g/7oz cans tuna, drained and
    flaked
30ml/2 tbsp chopped fresh parsley
salt and black pepper
lettuce leaves, to serve
thin strips twisted lemon rind,
    to garnish

1 Cut the radishes, cucumber, celery and yellow pepper into small cubes. Place in a large, shallow dish with the cherry tomatoes and spring onions.

2 In a small bowl, stir together the salt and lemon juice with a fork until dissolved. Pour this over the vegetable mixture. Add the oil and pepper to taste. Stir to coat the vegetables. Cover and set aside for 1 hour.

3 Add the flaked tuna and parsley to the mixture and toss gently until well combined.

4 Arrange the lettuce leaves on a platter and spoon the salad into the centre. Garnish with the lemon rind.

VARIATION
Prepare the vegetables as above and add the parsley. Arrange lettuce leaves on individual plates and divide the vegetable mixture among them. Place a mound of tuna on top of each and finish with a dollop of mayonnaise.

GOAT'S CHEESE TARTS

Serves 6

6–8 sheets filo pastry (about
   115g/4oz)
50g/2oz/4 tbsp butter, melted
350g/12oz firm goat's cheese
9 cherry tomatoes, quartered
120ml/4fl oz/½ cup milk
2 eggs
30ml/2 tbsp single cream
large pinch of white pepper

COOK'S TIP
Keep the filo pastry under a damp
cloth while working to prevent
the sheets from drying out.

---

1 First, preheat the oven to
190°C/375°F/Gas 5.

2 Grease six 10cm/4in tartlet tins.
Then for each tin, cut out four
rounds of filo pastry, each about
11.5cm/4½in in diameter. Place one
round in the tin and brush with butter.
Top with another filo round and
continue until there are four layers of
filo; do not butter the last layer. Repeat
for the remaining tins.

3 Place the pastry-lined tins on a
baking sheet. Cut the goat's cheese
log into six slices and place a slice of
cheese in each of the pastry cases.

4 Arrange the tomato quarters
around the goat's cheese slices.

5 Place the milk, eggs, cream and
pepper in a measuring jug or bowl
and whisk to mix. Pour into the pastry
cases, filling them almost to the top.

6 Bake in the oven for 30–40
minutes, until puffed and golden.
Serve hot or warm, with a mixed green
salad if desired.

TURKEY AND AVOCADO PITTA PIZZAS

INGREDIENTS

Serves 4

8 plum tomatoes, quartered
45–60ml/3–4 tbsp olive oil
1 large ripe avocado
8 small round pitta breads
6–7 slices cooked turkey, chopped
1 onion, very thinly sliced
275g/10oz/2½ cups grated
   Cheddar cheese
30ml/2 tbsp chopped fresh coriander
salt and black pepper

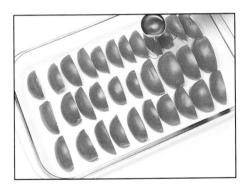

1 Preheat the oven to 230°C/450°F/ Gas 8. Place the tomatoes in a shallow ovenproof dish. Drizzle over 15ml/1 tbsp of the oil and season with salt and pepper. Bake for 30 minutes.

2 Mash the tomatoes with a fork, removing the skins as you mash. Set the tomatoes aside.

3 Halve, stone and peel the avocado, then cut into sixteen thin slices.

4 Brush the edges of the pitta breads with olive oil. Arrange the pitta breads on two baking sheets.

5 Spread each pitta with mashed tomato, almost to the edges.

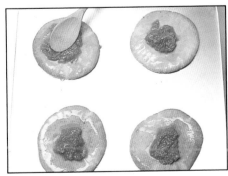

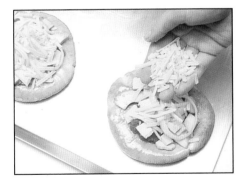

6 Top each with two avocado slices. Sprinkle with the turkey, then add a few onion slices and season with salt and pepper. Sprinkle on the cheese.

7 Bake the pitta pizzas for 15–20 minutes, until the cheese is golden. Sprinkle with the chopped coriander and serve hot.

MEXICAN MIXED SALAD

Serves 4
10ml/2 tsp vegetable oil
450g/1lb lean minced beef
1 small onion, chopped
1.25ml/¼ tsp cayenne pepper, or
to taste
200g/7oz can sweetcorn, drained
425g/15oz can kidney beans, drained
15ml/1 tbsp chopped fresh coriander,
plus extra coriander leaves, to garnish
1 small cos lettuce
3 tomatoes, sliced
225g/8oz/2 cups grated Cheddar cheese
1 avocado
50g/2oz stoned black olives, sliced
4 spring onions, chopped
salt and black pepper
tortilla chips, to serve

For the dressing
45ml/3 tbsp white wine vinegar
5ml/1 tsp Dijon mustard
30ml/2 tbsp single cream
150ml/¼ pint/⅔ cup vegetable oil
1 small garlic clove, finely chopped
5ml/1 tsp ground cumin
5ml/1 tsp dried oregano
salt and black pepper

VARIATIONS
For Chicken and Taco Salad, substitute 450g/1lb boneless, skinless chicken breast, finely diced, for the minced beef. Chick peas may be used in place of kidney beans. Although frozen or canned sweetcorn is convenient, freshly cooked sweetcorn kernels scraped from the cob give added moisture and extra flavour.

1 To make the dressing, mix the vinegar and salt with a fork until dissolved. Stir in the mustard and cream. Gradually stir in the oil until blended, then add the garlic, cumin, oregano and pepper and set aside.

2 Heat the oil in a large frying pan. Add the beef, onion, salt and cayenne and cook for 5–7 minutes, until just browned. Stir frequently to break up any lumps. Drain and leave to cool.

3 Place the beef mixture, sweetcorn, kidney beans and chopped coriander in a large bowl and toss to blend.

4 Stack the lettuce leaves on top of one another and slice thinly, crossways, into shreds. Place in another bowl and toss with 45ml/3 tbsp of the prepared dressing. Divide the lettuce among four serving plates.

5 Mound the meat mixture in the centre of the lettuce. Arrange the tomatoes at the edge and sprinkle with the grated cheese.

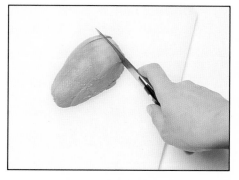

6 Halve, stone, peel and dice the avocado and add to salad. Scatter the olives and spring onions on top.

7 Pour the remaining dressing over the salads and garnish with coriander. Serve with tortilla chips.

CREAMY CREOLE CRAB

Serves 6

2 × 200g/7oz cans crab meat
3 hard-boiled eggs
5ml/1 tsp Dijon mustard
75g/3oz/6 tbsp butter or margarine, at
   room temperature
1.25ml/¼ tsp cayenne pepper
45ml/3 tbsp sherry
30ml/2 tbsp chopped fresh parsley
120ml/4fl oz/½ cup single or
   whipping cream
2–3 thinly sliced spring onions,
   including some of the green parts
50g/2oz/½ cup dried white
   breadcrumbs
salt and black pepper

1 Preheat the oven to 180°C/350°F/
Gas 4. Flake the crab meat into a
medium-sized bowl, keeping the pieces
of crab as large as possible and
removing any shell or cartilage.

2 In a medium-sized bowl, crumble
the egg yolks with a fork. Add the
mustard, 60ml/4 tbsp of the butter or
margarine and the cayenne pepper, then
mash together to form a paste. Mix in
the sherry and parsley.

3 Chop the egg whites and mix in
with the cream and spring onions.
Stir in the crab meat and season well.

4 Divide the crab mixture equally
among six greased scallop shells or
individual baking dishes. Sprinkle with
the breadcrumbs and dot with the
remaining butter or margarine.

5 Bake for about 20 minutes, until
bubbling hot and golden brown.

PRAWN SOUFFLÉ

INGREDIENTS

Serves 4–6

15ml/1 tbsp fine dried white
  breadcrumbs
25g/1oz/2 tbsp butter or margarine
175g/6oz cooked, peeled prawns,
  coarsely chopped
15ml/1 tbsp finely chopped fresh
  tarragon or parsley
45ml/3 tbsp sherry or dry
  white wine
black pepper

For the soufflé mixture

40g/1½oz/3 tbsp butter or margarine
37.5ml/2½ tbsp plain flour
250ml/8fl oz/1 cup milk, heated
4 eggs, separated, plus 1 white
salt

1 Butter a 1.5–1.75 litre/2½–3 pint soufflé dish. Sprinkle with the breadcrumbs, tilting the dish to coat the bottom and sides evenly. Preheat the oven to 200°C/400°F/Gas 6.

VARIATIONS
For Lobster Soufflé, substitute 1 large lobster tail for the cooked prawns. Chop it finely and add to the saucepan with the herbs and wine in place of the prawns. For Crab Soufflé, instead of prawns, use about 175g/6oz fresh crab meat or a 200g/7oz can, drained. Flake and pick over carefully to remove any bits of shell.

2 Melt the butter or margarine in a small saucepan. Add the chopped prawns and cook for 2–3 minutes over a low heat. Stir in the herbs, pepper and sherry or wine and cook for 1–2 minutes more. Raise the heat and boil rapidly to evaporate the liquid, then remove from the heat and set aside.

3 To make the soufflé mixture, melt the butter or margarine in a heavy-based saucepan. Add the flour, blending well with a wire whisk. Cook over a low heat for 2–3 minutes. Pour in the hot milk and whisk vigorously until smooth. Simmer for 2 minutes, still whisking, then season with salt.

4 Remove the pan from the heat and immediately beat in the egg yolks, one at a time. Stir in the prawn mixture.

5 Whisk the egg whites in a large bowl until they form stiff peaks. Stir about one-quarter of the egg whites into the prawn mixture, then gently fold in the rest of the egg whites.

6 Turn the mixture into the prepared dish. Place in the oven and reduce the temperature to 190°C/375°F/Gas 5. Bake for 30–40 minutes, until the soufflé is puffed up and lightly browned on top. Serve immediately.

GOAT'S CHEESE SALAD

INGREDIENTS

Serves 4

30ml/2 tbsp olive oil
4 thin slices of French bread
*mixed salad leaves, such as curly
    endive, radicchio and red oak leaf,
    torn in small pieces*
*4 firm goat's cheeses, about
    50g/2oz each*
*1 yellow or red pepper, seeded and
    finely diced*
1 small red onion, finely chopped
45ml/3 tbsp chopped fresh parsley
*30ml/2 tbsp chopped fresh chives plus a
    few whole chives, to garnish*

For the dressing

30ml/2 tbsp wine vinegar
5ml/1 tsp wholegrain mustard
75ml/5 tbsp olive oil
salt and black pepper

1 To make the dressing, mix the vinegar and a little salt with a fork until dissolved. Stir in the mustard, then gradually whisk in the oil. Season with pepper and set aside. Alternatively place all the dressing ingredients in a jar, put lid on tightly and shake well.

2 Heat the oil in a frying pan. When hot, add the bread slices and cook for about 1 minute until golden. Turn and cook on the other side for about 30 seconds more. Drain on kitchen paper and set aside. Preheat the grill.

3 Place the salad leaves in a bowl. Add 45ml/3 tbsp of the dressing and toss to coat. Divide the dressed leaves among four serving plates.

4 Put the goat's cheeses, cut side up, on a baking sheet and grill for 1–2 minutes, until bubbling and golden.

5 Arrange one cheese on each slice of fried bread and place in the centre of each plate. Scatter the diced pepper, red onion, parsley and chives over the salad. Drizzle with the remaining dressing, garnish with chives and serve.

VARIATION

For a more substantial main course salad, increase the amount of salad leaves and make double the quantity of dressing. Add 115g/4oz cooked green beans and 175g/6oz diced ham to the leaves and toss with half of the dressing. Top with the grilled goat's cheeses and the remaining dressing.

CHILLI BEAN DIP

Serves 4–6

250g/9oz/1½ cups dried pinto beans, soaked overnight in water and drained
1 bay leaf
15ml/1 tbsp vegetable oil
1 small onion, sliced
1 garlic clove, finely chopped
2–4 canned hot green chillies, seeded and chopped
85ml/3fl oz/⅓ cup soured cream, plus extra for serving
2.5ml/½ tsp ground cumin, plus extra for dusting
dash of Tabasco sauce
salt
tortilla chips, to serve

1 Place the beans in a large saucepan. Add fresh cold water to cover and the bay leaf. Bring to the boil and boil rapidly for 10 minutes, then reduce the heat, cover, and simmer for 20 minutes.

2 Add salt to taste, and continue simmering, covered, for 30 minutes until the beans are tender.

3 Drain the beans, reserving 120ml/ 4fl oz/½ cup of the cooking liquid. Leave to cool. Discard the bay leaf.

4 Heat the oil in a non-stick frying pan. Add the onion and garlic and cook over a low heat for 8–10 minutes, until just softened, stirring occasionally.

5 In a food processor or blender, combine the beans, onion mixture, chillies and the reserved cooking liquid. Process in short bursts until the mixture forms a coarse purée.

6 Transfer to a bowl and stir in the soured cream, ground cumin and Tabasco sauce. Garnish with extra soured cream and a dusting of cumin and serve warm with tortilla chips.

NUTTY DEVILLED EGGS

INGREDIENTS

Serves 6

9 hard-boiled eggs
50g/2oz/¼ cup finely chopped
*   cooked ham*
6 walnut halves, very finely chopped
15ml/1 tbsp very finely chopped
*   spring onion*
15ml/1 tbsp Dijon mustard
15ml/1 tbsp mayonnaise
10ml/2 tsp white wine vinegar
1.25ml/¼ tsp cayenne pepper
salt and black pepper
paprika and a few slices of dill pickle,
*   to garnish*

1 Cut each egg in half lengthways. Place the yolks in a bowl and set the whites aside.

2 Mash the yolks well with a fork, or push them through a sieve. Add all the remaining ingredients and mix well with the yolks. Season to taste with salt, pepper and cayenne.

3 Spoon the filling into the egg white halves, or pipe it in with a piping bag fitted with a wide nozzle. Sprinkle the top of each stuffed egg with a little paprika and garnish with a small piece of dill pickle. Serve the stuffed eggs at room temperature.

STUFFED CELERY STICKS

INGREDIENTS

Serves 4–6

12 celery sticks
25g/1oz/¼ cup crumbled blue cheese
115g/4oz/½ cup cream cheese
45ml/3 tbsp soured cream
50g/2oz/½ cup chopped walnuts

2 Place the crumbled blue cheese, cream cheese and soured cream in a small bowl. Stir together with a wooden spoon until smoothly blended. Fold in all but 15ml/1 tbsp of the chopped walnuts.

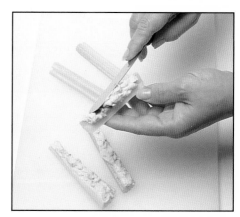

3 Fill the celery with the cheese mixture. Chill, then garnish with the reserved walnuts and celery leaves.

> **VARIATION**
> You could use the same filling to stuff scooped-out cherry tomatoes.

1 Cut the celery into 10cm/4in pieces. Reserve the leaves.

TOASTED TOMATO SANDWICHES

Serves 6

1 garlic clove, finely chopped
30ml/2 tbsp olive oil
5ml/1 tsp red wine vinegar
2 beefsteak tomatoes
60ml/4 tbsp chopped fresh basil leaves
*   or parsley*
7 stoned black olives, chopped
90ml/6 tbsp mayonnaise
12 slices of bread, lightly toasted
6 lettuce leaves
salt and black pepper

1 Mix together the finely chopped garlic, oil and vinegar in a small bowl and blend together. Alternatively, shake the ingredients in a screwtop jar until thoroughly blended. Set aside.

2 Cut out the cores from the tomatoes using a sharp knife.

3 Carefully cut three shallow lengthwise slits in the skin of each tomato to make them easier to eat; but do not cut too deeply into the flesh. Cut each of the tomatoes horizontally into five or six thin slices.

4 Place the tomato slices in a shallow dish. Add the oil and vinegar dressing, basil or parsley and salt and pepper to taste. Leave to marinate for at least 30 minutes.

5 Mix together the olives and mayonnaise in a separate bowl.

6 Spread six slices of toast with the olive mayonnaise. Arrange the tomato slices on top and drizzle over any remaining dressing from the bowl. Top each with a lettuce leaf. Cover with the remaining toast and serve.

BEETROOT AND CORNED BEEF HASH

Serves 4

6 streaky bacon rashers

1 onion, finely chopped

*450g/1lb potatoes, peeled, boiled and
    diced*

225g/8oz corned beef, chopped

*175g/6oz cooked beetroot (not in
    vinegar), diced*

50ml/2fl oz/¼ cup single cream

*45ml/3 tbsp finely chopped fresh
    parsley*

salt and black pepper

3 Heat 60ml/4 tbsp of the reserved
bacon fat, or other fat, in the frying
pan. Add the corned beef mixture,
spreading it evenly with a fish slice.
Cook over a low heat for about 15
minutes, until the base is brown. Tip the
hash upside down on to a plate.

4 Gently slide the hash back into the
frying pan and cook on the other
side until lightly browned. Serve the
hash immediately.

1 Cook the bacon in a large heavy-
based or non-stick frying pan until
golden and beginning to crisp. Remove
with a fish slice and drain on kitchen
paper. Pour all but 30ml/2 tbsp of the
bacon fat in the pan into a small jug and
reserve for later.

2 Cut the bacon into 1cm/½in pieces
and place in a mixing bowl. Cook
the onion in the bacon fat over low heat
for 8–10 minutes, until softened.
Remove it from the pan and add to the
bacon. Mix in the potatoes, corned
beef, beetroot, cream and chopped
parsley. Season with salt and black
pepper and mix well.

MEAT DISHES

There are main courses for every and any occasion in this section: warming stews and casseroles, such as Herby Beef Stew, to cook slowly on a winter's day; savoury beef and pork pot roasts for Sunday lunch; delicious dishes for when you are cooking family meals; and recipes for special occasions throughout the year. There are Pork Chops with Cider and Apples, and a wonderful Chilli Beef Pie for when you are entertaining informally, a Country Meat Loaf which will appeal to children and adults alike, and tender steaks and veal chops to serve at a dinner party. Mid-week meals are often cooked in a hurry, and there are quick and easy recipes too: meaty burgers with a melting blue cheese centre, meatballs to serve with a cream sauce, and a delicious and speedy Beef and Aubergine Stir-Fry.

CHILLI BEEF PIE

INGREDIENTS

Serves 8

115g/4oz bacon, chopped
1 onion, finely chopped
450g/1lb lean minced beef
10–15ml/2–3 tsp chilli powder
450g/1lb peeled fresh or canned
   tomatoes
50g/2oz/⅓ cup stoned black olives,
   chopped
200g/7oz can sweetcorn
120ml/4fl oz/½ cup soured cream
115g/4oz/1 cup grated Cheddar cheese
salt and black pepper

For the crust

250–300ml/8–10fl oz/1–1¼ cups
   chicken stock
175g/6oz/1½ cups polenta
75g/3oz/6 tbsp margarine
2.5ml/½ tsp baking powder
45ml/3 tbsp milk
salt and black pepper

1 Preheat the oven to 190°C/375°F/
Gas 5. Cook the bacon for 2–3
minutes in a large frying pan until the
fat runs. Pour off the excess fat, leaving
15–30ml/1–2 tbsp. Add the chopped
onion and cook for about 5 minutes
until just softened.

2 Add the beef, chilli powder and salt
and pepper and cook for 5 minutes,
stirring to break up the meat. Stir in the
tomatoes and cook for 5 minutes more,
breaking them up with a spoon.

3 Add the olives, sweetcorn and
soured cream and mix well.
Transfer to a large rectangular or oval
baking dish. Set aside.

4 To make the crust, bring the stock
to the boil in a saucepan and season
with salt and pepper.

5 In a food processor, combine the
polenta, margarine, baking powder
and milk and process until combined.
With the machine on, gradually pour in
the hot stock until a smooth, thick
batter is obtained. If the batter is too
thick to spread, add more hot stock or
water, a little at a time, keeping the
machine running all the time.

6 Pour the batter over the top of the
beef mixture, spreading it evenly
with a metal spatula.

7 Bake for about 20 minutes until the
top is just browned. Sprinkle the
surface evenly with the grated cheese
and continue baking for 10–15 minutes
more until the cheese is melted and
bubbling. Serve hot with a salad.

POT-ROAST PORK WITH RED CABBAGE

Serves 8
2kg/4½lb boned loin of pork
2.5ml/½ tsp ground ginger
50g/2oz/4 tbsp butter, melted
about 350ml/12fl oz/1½ cups sweet
    cider or dry white wine
salt and black pepper

For the cabbage
65g/2½oz/3 tbsp butter or margarine
1 large onion, finely sliced
5ml/1 tsp caraway seeds
3 tart eating apples, quartered, cored
    and sliced
15ml/1 tbsp soft dark brown sugar
1.5kg/3½lb red cabbage, cored and
    shredded
90ml/6 tbsp cider vinegar, or 60ml/
    4 tbsp wine vinegar and 30ml/2 tbsp
    water
120ml/4fl oz/½ cup beef stock
120ml/4fl oz/½ cup sweet cider or
    white wine
5ml/1 tsp salt
1.25ml/¼ tsp dried thyme leaves
fresh parsley sprigs, to garnish

2 Place the pork, fat side down, in a large flameproof casserole. Cook over a medium heat, turning frequently for about 15 minutes, until browned on all sides. Add a little of the melted butter if the meat starts to stick.

3 Cover the casserole, transfer to the oven and roast for 1 hour, basting frequently with the meat juices, melted butter and cider or wine.

4 Meanwhile, prepare the cabbage; melt the butter or margarine in a large frying pan and add the onion and caraway seeds. Cook over a low heat for 8–10 minutes until softened, stirring occasionally. Stir in the apple slices and brown sugar. Cover the pan and cook for a further 4–5 minutes.

5 Stir in the cabbage and add the vinegar. Cover and cook for 10 minutes. Pour in the stock and cider or wine, add the salt and thyme leaves and stir well. Cover again and cook over a medium-low heat for 30 minutes.

6 When the pork has cooked for 1 hour, remove from the oven. Transfer the pork to a plate and keep warm. Tilt the casserole and spoon off all but 30ml/2 tbsp of the fat.

7 Transfer the cabbage mixture from the frying pan to the casserole and stir well to mix the cabbage thoroughly with the roasting juices.

8 Place the pork on the cabbage, cover and return to the oven. Cook for another hour, basting occasionally. Serve garnished with fresh parsley.

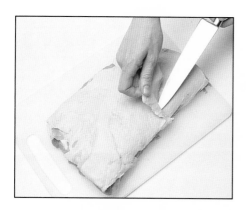

1 Preheat the oven to 180°C/350°F/ Gas 4. Trim any excess fat from the pork and tie it into a neat shape using fine string. Sprinkle with the ground ginger and salt and pepper.

Pork Chops with Cider and Apples

INGREDIENTS

Serves 4

3–4 small cooking apples, peeled,
quartered and cored
4 pork chops, about 2.5cm/1in thick
5ml/1 tsp dried thyme
1.25ml/¼ tsp ground allspice
15g/½oz/1tbsp butter
15ml/1 tbsp vegetable oil
1 bay leaf
120ml/4fl oz/½ cup cider
30ml/2 tbsp single cream
salt and black pepper
potato fritters, to serve

1 Preheat the oven to 190°C/375°F/ Gas 5. Grease a large shallow ovenproof dish.

2 Arrange the apples in a single layer in the prepared dish. Set aside.

3 Sprinkle the pork chops on both sides with the thyme, ground allspice and a little salt and pepper.

4 Heat the butter and oil in a frying pan. Add the pork chops and cook over a medium-high heat for 2–3 minutes, until browned. Turn the chops over and cook the other sides for 2–3 minutes more until browned.

5 Arrange the pork chops on top of the apples. Add the bay leaf and pour over the cider. Cover the dish and bake for 15 minutes.

6 Turn the chops over. Continue baking for about 15 minutes more, until they are cooked through.

7 Transfer the pork chops to four warmed plates. Remove the apple quarters with a slotted spoon and divide them equally among the plates.

8 Stir the cream and pork juices into the frying pan. Heat until warmed through. Adjust seasoning. Spoon the sauce over the chops and serve immediately, with potato fritters.

PORK BRAISED IN BEER

INGREDIENTS

Serves 6

1.75–2.25kg/4–5¼lb loin of pork,
boned, trimmed of excess fat and tied
15ml/1 tbsp butter
15ml/1 tbsp vegetable oil
3 large onions, halved and thinly sliced
1 garlic clove, finely chopped
600ml/1 pint/2½ cups beer
1 bay leaf
15ml/1 tbsp plain flour blended with
30ml/2 tbsp water
salt and black pepper
courgettes, to serve

1 Season the pork on all sides with salt and pepper. Heat the butter and oil in a flameproof casserole just large enough to hold the pork. When hot, add the pork and brown on all sides for 5–7 minutes, turning it to colour evenly. Remove from the casserole and set aside.

2 Drain all but 15ml/1 tbsp fat from the casserole. Add the onions and garlic and cook for about 5 minutes, until just softened.

3 Stir in the beer, scraping to remove any bits on the bottom of the casserole. Add the bay leaf.

4 Return the pork to the casserole. Cover and cook over a low heat for about 2 hours, turning the pork halfway through the cooking time.

5 Remove the pork from the casserole. Slice thickly. Arrange on a platter. Cover and keep warm.

6 Discard the bay leaf. Add the flour mixture to the cooking juices and cook over a high heat, stirring constantly, until thickened. Taste for seasoning. Pour over the pork and serve at once with courgettes.

COUNTRY MEAT LOAF

INGREDIENTS

Serves 6

25g/1oz/2 tbsp butter or margarine
½ onion, finely chopped
2 garlic cloves, finely chopped
2 celery sticks, finely chopped
450g/1lb lean minced beef
225g/8oz minced veal
225g/8oz lean minced pork
2 eggs
50g/2oz/1 cup fresh white
   breadcrumbs
90ml/6 tbsp chopped fresh parsley
30ml/2 tbsp chopped fresh basil
2.5ml/½ tsp fresh or dried thyme
30ml/2 tbsp Worcestershire sauce
45ml/3 tbsp chilli sauce
6 streaky bacon rashers
salt and black pepper
fresh basil and parsley sprigs,
   to garnish

1 Preheat the oven to 180°C/350°F/ Gas 4. Melt the butter or margarine in a small frying pan over a low heat. Add the onion, garlic and celery and cook for 8–10 minutes, until softened. Remove the frying pan from the heat and leave to cool slightly.

2 Tip the onion mixture into a large bowl and add all the other ingredients except the bacon. Mix together lightly, using a fork or your fingers. Do not overwork or the meat loaf will be too compact.

3 Form the meat mixture into an oval loaf. Carefully transfer it to a shallow baking tin.

4 Lay the bacon rashers across the meat loaf. Bake for 1¼ hours, basting occasionally with the juices and bacon fat in the tin. Remove the meat loaf from the oven and drain off the fat. Leave to stand for 10 minutes. Garnish with basil and parsley and serve.

MEATBALLS WITH CREAM SAUCE

INGREDIENTS

Serves 6

25g/1oz/2 tbsp butter or margarine
½ onion, finely chopped
350g/12oz minced beef
115g/4oz minced veal
225g/8oz lean minced pork
1 egg
115g/4oz cooked mashed potatoes
30ml/2 tbsp chopped fresh dill
    or parsley
1 garlic clove, finely chopped
2.5ml/½ tsp ground allspice
1.25ml/¼ tsp grated nutmeg
40g/1½oz/¾ cup fresh white
    breadcrumbs
175ml/6fl oz/¾ cup milk
about 40g/1½oz/⅓ cup plain flour
30ml/2 tbsp olive oil
175ml/6fl oz/¾ cup single cream
salt and black pepper
fresh dill sprigs, to garnish
buttered tagliatelle, to serve

3 Put the breadcrumbs in a small bowl and add the milk. Stir until well moistened, then add to the other ingredients and mix well.

4 Shape the mixture into balls about 2.5cm/1in in diameter. Roll them in some of the flour to coat evenly.

5 Heat the oil in the pan over a medium heat. Add the meatballs and cook for 8–10 minutes until brown on all sides, shaking the pan occasionally so the balls colour evenly.

6 With a slotted spoon, remove the meatballs to a serving dish. Cover with foil and keep warm.

7 Stir 15ml/1 tbsp of flour into the fat in the frying pan. Add the cream and mix in with a small whisk. Simmer for 3–4 minutes. Taste to check the seasoning and adjust if necessary. Serve the meatballs on a bed of buttered tagliatelle with the sauce poured over. Garnish with dill.

COOK'S TIP
The meatballs are also good, served without the sauce, and speared with cocktail sticks for a buffet or drinks party.

1 Melt the butter or margarine in a large frying pan. Add the onion and cook over low heat for 8–10 minutes, until softened. Remove from the heat. Transfer the onion to a large mixing bowl using a slotted spoon.

2 Add the minced beef, veal and pork, the egg, mashed potatoes, dill or parsley, garlic, allspice, nutmeg and salt and pepper to the bowl.

BEEF AND AUBERGINE STIR-FRY

INGREDIENTS

Serves 4–6
600g/1lb 5oz rump steak, thinly sliced
30ml/2 tbsp soy sauce, plus extra
    to serve
450g/1lb aubergines
45ml/3 tbsp water
30ml/2 tbsp rice vinegar
15ml/1 tbsp dry sherry
5ml/1 tsp honey
5ml/1 tsp dried red pepper flakes
50ml/2fl oz/¼ cup vegetable oil
15ml/1 tbsp sesame oil
1 garlic clove, finely chopped
15ml/1 tbsp fresh root ginger, finely
    chopped
salt and black pepper
boiled rice, to serve
fresh parsley sprigs, to garnish

1 Mix together the beef and soy sauce in a shallow dish and stir to coat evenly. Cover and leave to marinate for 1 hour, or chill overnight.

VARIATION
For Turkey and Aubergine Stir-Fry, substitute thinly sliced turkey breast for the beef. If time is short, it is not essential to precook the aubergine, but microwaving or steaming it before stir-frying helps to eliminate any bitterness and also prevents it from soaking up too much oil.

2 Cut the aubergine into eight lengths. Trim away the inner part with the seeds and discard, leaving a flat edge. Then cut the aubergine slices on the diagonal into diamond shapes that are about 2.5cm/1in wide.

3 Place the aubergine pieces in a large microwave-proof dish and add the water. Cover and microwave on high for 3 minutes. Stir, cover and microwave for a further 3 minutes. Set aside, still covered. (Alternatively, steam the aubergine pieces over boiling water until tender.)

4 Place the vinegar, sherry, honey and pepper flakes in a small bowl and stir to mix. Set aside.

5 Heat 15ml/1 tbsp vegetable oil and 5ml/1 tsp sesame oil in a large non-stick frying pan or wok. Add half the marinated beef, garlic and ginger. Cook over a high heat for 2–3 minutes, stirring frequently, until the beef is just cooked through. Transfer to a bowl. Cook the remaining beef, garlic and ginger in the same way. Add to the cooked beef and set aside.

6 Heat the remaining vegetable and sesame oils in the frying pan or wok. Add the aubergine and cook over a moderate heat for about 5 minutes until just browned and tender, frying them in two batches, if necessary.

7 Return the beef to the pan or wok. Stir in the vinegar mixture and cook for 2–3 minutes, or until the liquid is absorbed. Taste for seasoning and adjust if necessary. Serve immediately, with rice, garnished with parsley and accompanied by extra soy sauce.

BLUE CHEESE BURGERS

INGREDIENTS

Serves 4

1kg/2lb lean minced beef
1 garlic clove, crushed
30ml/2 tbsp chopped fresh parsley
30ml/2 tbsp chopped fresh chives
2.5ml/½ tsp salt
225g/8oz blue cheese, crumbled
4 hamburger buns, split and toasted
black pepper
tomato slices and lettuce, to serve
mustard or tomato ketchup,
    to serve

1 Place the beef, garlic, parsley, chives, salt and a little pepper in a bowl. Mix lightly together, then form into four thick burgers.

2 Make a slit in the side of each burger, poking well into the beef to form a pocket. Fill each pocket with 50g/2oz of the blue cheese.

3 Close up the holes to seal the blue cheese inside the burgers.

4 Heat a ridged heavy-based frying pan. Cook the burgers for 4–5 minutes on each side for medium-rare, and 6–7 minutes for well-done. Alternatively, cook the burgers under a grill, turning once.

5 Place the burgers in the toasted and split hamburger buns. Serve with sliced tomatoes and lettuce leaves, and mustard or tomato ketchup.

STEAK WITH MUSHROOMS AND LEEKS

INGREDIENTS

Serves 4

6–8 baby leeks (about 500g/1¼lb), white and light green parts only
60ml/4 tbsp olive oil
675g/1½lb mushrooms, quartered
475ml/16fl oz/2 cups dry red wine, such as a Pinot Noir or Merlot
4 × 225g/8oz sirloin steaks, about 2cm/¾in thick
15ml/1 tbsp chopped fresh parsley
salt and freshly ground black pepper

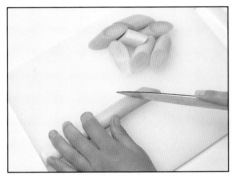

1 Trim the leeks and cut into 2.5cm/1in slices on the diagonal.

2 Heat 45ml/3 tbsp of the oil in a large frying pan. When hot, add the leeks and mushrooms and cook over a medium heat for 3–4 minutes, stirring frequently, until lightly browned.

3 Stir in the wine, scraping the bottom of the pan. Season with salt and pepper. Bring to the boil and boil 1 minute. Reduce the heat to low, then cover and cook for 5 minutes.

4 Remove the lid, raise the heat, and cook for about 5 minutes, until the wine has reduced slightly. Set aside.

5 Brush the steaks with the remaining 15ml/1 tbsp oil and sprinkle generously on both sides with salt and freshly ground black pepper.

6 Heat a ridged heavy-based frying pan. When hot, add the steaks and cook for 3–4 minutes on each side for medium-rare. Alternatively, cook the steaks under the grill, turning once.

7 Meanwhile, stir the parsley into the leek mixture and reheat. Place the steaks on four warmed serving plates. Scatter the leek mixture on top and serve at once.

> **COOK'S TIP**
> If available, use a variety of mushrooms for extra flavour.

HERBY BEEF STEW

Serves 6

60ml/4 tbsp vegetable oil
2 onions, chopped
4 large carrots, thickly sliced
1.5kg/3lb braising steak, cubed
20g/¾oz/3 tbsp plain flour
750ml/1¼ pints/3 cups unsalted
  beef stock
250ml/8fl oz/1 cup strong black coffee
10ml/2 tsp dried oregano
1 bay leaf
115g/4oz fresh or frozen peas
salt and black pepper
mashed potatoes, to serve

1 Heat 30ml/2 tbsp of the oil in a large saucepan. Add the onions and carrots and cook over a medium heat for about 8 minutes, until softened and lightly browned. Remove the vegetables with a slotted spoon, transfer to a plate or dish and reserve.

2 Add another 15ml/1 tbsp of oil to the pan and add the beef cubes. Increase the heat and cook until browned all over. If necessary, fry the meat in batches to ensure it browns evenly. Season to taste.

3 Return the vegetables to the pan and stir in the flour and the remaining oil. Cook, stirring constantly, for 1 minute. Add the beef stock, coffee, oregano and bay leaf. Bring to the boil and cook, stirring often, until thickened. Reduce the heat to very low. Cover the pan and allow the stew to simmer very gently for 1–1½ hours until the beef is tender.

4 Add the peas and simmer for a further 5–10 minutes. Discard the bay leaf and taste and adjust seasoning. Serve hot with mashed potatoes.

VEAL CHOPS WITH CARROTS

—— INGREDIENTS ——

Serves 4
15ml/1 tbsp vegetable oil
15g/½oz/1 tbsp butter
4 veal chops, about 2cm/¾in thick
1 onion, thinly sliced
120ml/4fl oz/½ cup dry white wine
675g/1½lb carrots, cut into
    1cm/½in slices
1 bay leaf
120ml/4fl oz/½ cup single cream
salt and black pepper
parsley sprigs, to garnish

1 Preheat the oven to 180°C/350°F/ Gas 4. Heat the oil and butter in a large flameproof casserole. Add the chops and cook over a medium heat for 6–8 minutes, until well browned on both sides. Transfer to a plate, season and set aside.

3 Return the chops to the casserole. Add the carrots, season with salt and pepper and add the bay leaf.

4 Cover the casserole and transfer to the oven. Cook for about 30 minutes, until the chops are tender.

5 Transfer the chops and carrots to warmed plates, cover and keep warm. Discard the bay leaf. Stir the cream into the cooking liquid and bring to the boil. Simmer the sauce for 2–3 minutes, until slightly thickened.

2 Add the onion to the casserole and cook for about 5 minutes, until just softened. Stir in the wine.

6 Season the sauce if necessary, then spoon over the chops. Serve at once, garnished with fresh parsley.

BEEF POT ROAST

INGREDIENTS

Serves 8

*1.75kg/4lb joint beef suitable for pot
    roasting, such as brisket*
3 garlic cloves, cut in half or in thirds
225g/8oz piece salt pork or bacon
275g/10oz/2 cups onions, chopped
3 celery sticks, chopped
2 carrots, chopped
115g/4oz turnip, diced
*475ml/16fl oz/2 cups beef or
    chicken stock*
*475ml/16fl oz/2 cups dry red or
    white wine*
1 bay leaf
*5ml/1 tsp fresh thyme, or 2.5ml/¹/₂ tsp
    dried*
*4–6 small whole potatoes, or 3 large
    potatoes, quartered*
*50g/2oz/4 tbsp butter or margarine, at
    room temperature*
25g/1oz/¹/₄ cup plain flour
salt and black pepper
watercress, to garnish

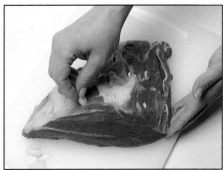

1 Preheat the oven to 160°C/325°F/
Gas 3. Make deep incisions in the
beef joint on all sides with the tip of a
small sharp knife and insert the garlic
pieces.

2 In a large flameproof casserole,
cook the salt pork or bacon over a
low heat until the fat runs and the pork
or bacon begins to brown.

3 Remove the salt pork with a slotted
spoon and discard. Increase the
heat to medium-high and add the beef
joint. Brown it evenly on all sides.
Remove and set aside on a plate or dish.

4 Add the onions, celery and carrots
to the casserole and cook for 8–10
minutes, until softened. Stir in the
turnips, add the stock, wine and herbs
and mix well. Return the joint and any
juices to the casserole, cover and cook
in the oven for 2 hours.

5 Add the potatoes to the casserole,
pushing them down under the
other vegetables. Season with salt and
pepper. Cover and cook for about 45
minutes, until the potatoes are tender.

6 Combine the butter or margarine
with the flour in a small bowl and
mash together to make a paste.

7 Transfer the meat to a warmed
serving dish. Remove the potatoes
and other vegetables from the casserole
with a slotted spoon and arrange
around the joint. Keep warm.

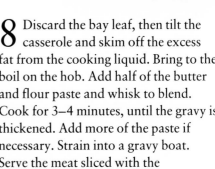

8 Discard the bay leaf, then tilt the
casserole and skim off the excess
fat from the cooking liquid. Bring to the
boil on the hob. Add half of the butter
and flour paste and whisk to blend.
Cook for 3–4 minutes, until the gravy is
thickened. Add more of the paste if
necessary. Strain into a gravy boat.
Serve the meat sliced with the
vegetables and the sauce poured over.
Garnish with watercress.

VARIATION
Add 175g/6oz frozen peas to the
casserole about 5 minutes before
the potatoes are cooked.

POULTRY AND GAME

Chicken and turkey are increasingly popular family foods as they appeal to both the young and not so young, and, as the meat is relatively low in fat, are light to eat and healthy to boot. This delicious collection of dishes from around the world includes recipes that are incredibly quick to cook such as Cajun-Spiced Chicken and Pasta with Turkey and Tomatoes; crisp and finger-lickingly tasty Oven-Fried Chicken; slow-cooked Chicken, Pepper and Bean Stew; an excellent Chicken and Mushroom Pie; and roasts, such as Poussin with Raisin Stuffing, for weekend meals. There's plenty of choice for entertaining, too. Try the deliciously different Lemon Chicken with Guacamole Sauce, opt for the more traditional Chicken with White Wine or choose Rabbit with Parsley Sauce.

TURKEY BREASTS WITH TOMATO SALSA

Serves 4

4 skinless boneless turkey breast fillets,
  about 175g/6oz each
30ml/2 tbsp fresh lemon juice
30ml/2 tbsp olive oil
2.5ml/1/2 tsp ground cumin
2.5ml/1/2 tsp dried oregano
salt and coarsely ground black pepper

For the salsa

1 fresh green chilli
450g/1lb tomatoes, seeded
  and chopped
200g/7oz can sweetcorn, drained
3 spring onions, chopped
15ml/1 tbsp finely chopped fresh
  parsley
30ml/2 tbsp finely chopped fresh
  coriander
30ml/2 tbsp fresh lemon juice
45ml/3 tbsp olive oil
salt, to taste

1 Pound the turkey breasts with a meat mallet, breasts between two sheets of greaseproof paper, until thin.

VARIATION
Use the cooked turkey, thinly sliced and combined with the salsa, as a filling for pancakes.

2 Blend the lemon juice, oil, cumin, oregano and pepper in a shallow dish. Add the turkey and turn to coat. Cover and leave to stand for at least 2 hours, or chill overnight.

3 To make the salsa, roast the chilli over a gas flame, holding it with tongs, until charred on all sides. (Alternatively, char the skin under the grill.) Leave to cool for 5 minutes. Wearing rubber gloves, carefully rub off the charred skin. For a less fiery salsa, discard the seeds. Chop the chilli finely and place in a bowl.

4 Add all the remaining salsa ingredients to the chilli and stir well until mixed thoroughly. Set aside.

5 Remove the turkey breast fillets from the marinade. Season lightly on both sides with salt to taste.

6 Heat a heavy-based ridged frying pan. When hot, add the turkey breasts and cook for about 3 minutes, until browned. Turn and cook the meat on the other side for a further 3–4 minutes, until cooked through. Serve immediately with the salsa.

CHICKEN WITH WHITE WINE AND OLIVES

—— INGREDIENTS ——

Serves 4

1.5kg/3¹/₂lb chicken, cut into pieces
1 onion, sliced
3–6 garlic cloves, finely chopped
5ml/1 tsp dried thyme
475ml/16fl oz/2 cups dry white wine
16–18 stoned green olives
1 bay leaf
15ml/1 tbsp fresh lemon juice
15–25g/¹/₂–1oz/1–2 tbsp butter
black pepper
fresh bay leaves and lemon rind,
  to garnish

1 Heat a large, heavy-based frying pan. When hot, add the chicken pieces, skin-side down, and cook over a medium heat for about 10 minutes, until browned. Turn over the chicken pieces and brown the other side for 5–8 minutes more.

2 Transfer the chicken pieces to a platter and set aside.

3 Drain the excess fat from the pan, leaving about 15ml/1 tbsp. Add the sliced onion and 2.5ml/¹/₂ tsp salt and cook for about 5 minutes, until just soft. Add the garlic and thyme and cook for a further 1 minute.

4 Add the wine and stir, scraping up any bits that cling to the pan. Bring to the boil and boil for about 1 minute, then stir in the green olives.

5 Return the chicken pieces to the pan. Add the bay leaf and season lightly with pepper. Reduce the heat, cover and simmer for 20–30 minutes, until the chicken is cooked through.

6 Transfer the chicken pieces to a warm serving dish. Stir the lemon juice into the sauce and whisk in the butter to thicken the sauce slightly. Spoon the sauce over the chicken and serve at once, garnished with bay leaves and lemon rind.

TURKEY MEAT LOAF

—— INGREDIENTS ——

Serves 4

15ml/1 tbsp olive oil
1 onion, chopped
1 green pepper, seeded and finely
  chopped
1 garlic clove, finely chopped
450g/1lb minced turkey
50g/2oz/1 cup fresh white breadcrumbs
1 egg, beaten
50g/2oz/¹/₂ cup pine nuts
12 sun-dried tomatoes in oil, drained
  and chopped
85ml/3fl oz/¹/₃ cup milk
10ml/2 tsp chopped fresh rosemary or
  2.5ml/¹/₂ tsp dried
5ml/1 tsp fennel seeds
2.5ml/¹/₂ tsp dried oregano
salt and black pepper

1 Preheat the oven to 190°C/375°F/ Gas 5. Heat the oil in a frying pan. Add the onion, green pepper and garlic and cook over a low heat for 8–10 minutes, stirring frequently, until the vegetables are just softened. Remove from the heat and leave to cool.

2 Place the minced turkey in a large bowl. Add the onion mixture and all the remaining ingredients and mix together thoroughly.

3 Transfer to a 21 × 11cm/8¹/₂ × 4¹/₂in loaf tin, packing down firmly. Bake for about 1 hour, until golden brown. Serve with a salad.

RABBIT WITH PARSLEY SAUCE

Serves 4

90ml/6 tbsp soy sauce
few drops of Tabasco sauce
5ml/1 tsp sweet paprika
5ml/1 tsp dried basil
1–1.5kg/2–3lb rabbit, cut into pieces
45ml/3 tbsp peanut or olive oil
75g/3oz/¾ cup plain flour
1 large onion, finely sliced
250ml/8fl oz/1 cup dry white wine
250ml/8fl oz/1 cup chicken stock
2 cloves garlic, finely chopped
60ml/4 tbsp fresh chopped parsley
salt and white pepper
mashed potatoes or rice, to serve
fresh parsley sprigs, to garnish

1 Combine the soy sauce, Tabasco sauce, white pepper, paprika, and basil in a medium-sized bowl. Add the rabbit pieces and turn them over in the mixture so they are coated thoroughly. Let marinate at least 1 hour.

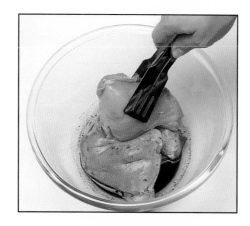

2 Heat the oil in a flameproof casserole. Coat the rabbit pieces lightly in the flour, shaking off the excess. Brown the rabbit pieces in the hot oil for about 5–6 minutes, turning them frequently. Remove the rabbit pieces with a slotted spoon and set aside on a plate or dish. Preheat the oven to 180°C/350°F/Gas 4.

3 Add the onion to the casserole and cook over a low heat for 8–10 minutes, until softened. Increase the heat, add the wine, and stir well to mix in all the cooking juices.

4 Return the rabbit and any juices to the casserole. Add the stock, garlic, parsley and salt. Mix well and turn the rabbit to coat with the sauce. Cover and place in the oven. Cook for about 1 hour, until the rabbit is tender, stirring occasionally. Serve garnished with parsley sprigs and accompanied by mashed potatoes or rice.

CAJUN-SPICED CHICKEN

INGREDIENTS

Serves 6

6 medium skinless boneless
  chicken breasts
75g/3oz/6 tbsp butter or margarine
5ml/1 tsp garlic powder
10ml/2 tsp onion powder
5ml/2 tsp cayenne pepper
10ml/2 tsp paprika
7.5ml/1½ tsp salt
2.5ml/½ tsp white pepper
5ml/1 tsp black pepper
1.25ml/¼ tsp ground cumin
5ml/1 tsp dried thyme
salad leaves and pepper strips,
  to garnish

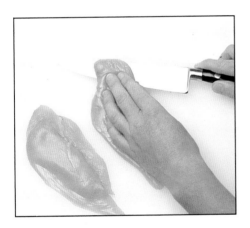

1 Slice each chicken breast in half horizontally, making two pieces of about the same thickness. Flatten them slightly with the heel of your hand.

2 Melt the butter or margarine in a small saucepan over a low heat.

VARIATION
For Cajun-Spiced Fish substitute six white fish fillets for the chicken. Do not slice in half, but season as for the chicken and cook for 2 minutes on one side and 1½–2 minutes on the other, until the fish flakes easily.

3 Combine all the remaining ingredients in a bowl and stir to blend well. Brush the chicken pieces on both sides with a little of the melted butter or margarine, then sprinkle evenly with the seasoning mixture.

4 Heat a large heavy-based frying pan over high heat for about 5–8 minutes, until a drop of water sprinkled on the surface sizzles.

5 Drizzle 5ml/1 tsp melted butter on to each chicken piece. Place them in the frying pan in an even layer, two or three at a time, and cook for 2–3 minutes, until the underside begins to blacken. Turn and cook the other side for 2–3 minutes more. Serve hot with salad leaves and pepper strips.

LEMON CHICKEN WITH GUACAMOLE SAUCE

———— INGREDIENTS ————

Serves 4
juice of 2 lemons
45ml/3 tbsp olive oil
2 garlic cloves, finely chopped
4 chicken breasts, about 200g/7oz each
2 large tomatoes, cored and cut in half
chopped fresh coriander, to garnish
salt and black pepper

For the sauce
1 ripe avocado
60ml/4 tbsp soured cream
45ml/3 tbsp fresh lemon juice
2.5ml/½ tsp salt
50ml/2fl oz/¼ cup water

2 Arrange the chicken breasts, in one layer, in a shallow glass or ceramic dish. Pour over the lemon mixture and turn to coat evenly. Cover and leave to stand for at least 1 hour at room temperature, or chill overnight.

5 Preheat the grill and heat a ridged frying pan. Remove the chicken from the marinade and pat dry.

1 Combine the lemon juice, oil, garlic, 2.5ml/½ tsp salt and a little pepper in a bowl. Stir to mix.

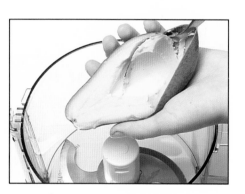

3 To make the sauce, halve the avocado, remove the stone and scrape the flesh into a food processor.

6 When the frying pan is hot, add the chicken breasts and cook for about 10 minutes, turning them frequently, until they are cooked through.

VARIATION
To barbecue the chicken, prepare the fire, and when the coals are glowing red and covered with grey ash, spread them in a single layer. Set an oiled rack about 13cm/5in above the coals and cook the chicken breasts for about 15–20 minutes until lightly charred and cooked through, brushing with oil, to baste.

4 Add the soured cream, lemon juice and salt and process until smooth. Add the water and process just to blend. If necessary, add a little more water to thin the sauce. Transfer to a bowl, taste and adjust the seasoning if necessary. Set aside in a cool place.

7 Meanwhile, arrange the tomato halves, cut-sides up, on a baking sheet and season lightly with salt and black pepper. Grill for about 5 minutes, until hot and bubbling.

8 To serve, place a chicken breast, tomato half and a dollop of avocado sauce on each plate. Sprinkle with chopped coriander and serve.

SPICY ROAST CHICKEN

Serves 4

1.5kg/3½lb chicken
juice of 1 lemon
4 garlic cloves, finely chopped
15ml/1 tbsp each cayenne pepper,
*   paprika, dried oregano*
10ml/2 tsp olive oil
salt and black pepper
fresh coriander sprigs, to garnish
mixed sliced peppers, to serve

COOK'S TIP
Roasting chicken in an oven that
has not been preheated produces a
particularly crispy skin.

---

1 With a sharp knife or poultry
shears, remove the backbone from
the chicken. Turn it breast-side up.
With the heel of your hand, press down
to break the breastbone and open the
chicken out flat like a book. Insert a
skewer through the chicken, at the
thighs, to keep it flat during cooking.

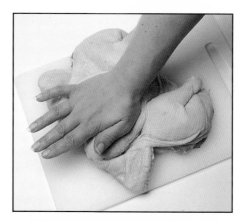

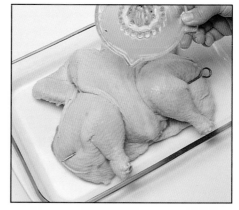

2 Place the chicken in a shallow dish
and pour over the lemon juice.

3 Place the garlic, cayenne, paprika,
oregano, pepper and oil in a small
bowl and mix well. Rub evenly over
the surface of the chicken. Cover and
leave to marinate for 2–3 hours at
room temperature, or chill the chicken
overnight and return to room
temperature before roasting.

4 Season both sides of the chicken
with salt and place it, skin side up,
in a shallow roasting tin.

5 Put the tin in a cold oven and set
the temperature to 200°C/400°F/
Gas 6. Roast for about 1 hour, until the
chicken is done basting with the juices
in the tin. To test whether the chicken is
cooked, prick the thickest part of the
flesh with a skewer: the juices that run
out should be clear. Serve hot,
garnished with coriander sprigs and
served with mixed sweet peppers.

PASTA WITH TURKEY AND TOMATOES

Serves 4

675g/1½lb ripe but firm plum
  tomatoes, quartered
90ml/6 tbsp olive oil
5ml/1 tsp dried oregano
350g/12oz broccoli florets
1 small onion, sliced
5ml/1 tsp dried thyme
450g/1lb turkey breast fillets, cubed
3 garlic cloves, finely chopped
15ml/1 tbsp fresh lemon juice
350g/12oz dried pasta twists
salt and black pepper

4 Heat 30ml/2 tbsp of the remaining oil in a large non-stick frying pan. Add the onion, thyme, turkey and salt, to taste. Cook over a high heat for 5–7 minutes, stirring frequently, until the meat is cooked and beginning to brown. Add the garlic and cook for a further 1 minute, stirring frequently.

5 Remove from the heat. Stir in the lemon juice and season with pepper. Set aside and keep warm.

6 Bring another large pan of salted water to the boil. Add the pasta and cook for 10–12 minutes, until just tender. Drain and place in a large serving bowl. Toss the pasta with the remaining oil.

7 Add the broccoli to the turkey mixture and toss into the pasta. Peel the tomatoes and stir gently into the pasta mixture. Serve immediately.

1 Preheat the oven to 200°C/400°F/ Gas 6. Place the tomatoes in a baking dish. Drizzle over 15ml/1 tbsp of the oil, scatter over the oregano and season with salt.

2 Bake for 30–40 minutes, until the tomatoes are just browned.

3 Meanwhile, bring a large pan of salted water to the boil. Add the broccoli and cook for about 5 minutes, until just tender. Drain the broccoli and set aside. Alternatively, steam the broccoli until tender.

CHICKEN, PEPPER AND BEAN STEW

INGREDIENTS

Serves 4–6

1.75kg/4lb chicken, cut into pieces
paprika
30ml/2 tbsp olive oil
25g/1oz/2 tbsp butter
2 onions, chopped
½ each green and yellow
  pepper, chopped
450g/1lb/2 cups peeled, chopped, fresh
  or canned plum tomatoes
250ml/8fl oz/1 cup white wine
475ml/16fl oz/2 cups chicken stock
  or water
45ml/3 tbsp chopped fresh parsley
2.5ml/½ tsp Tabasco sauce
15ml/1 tbsp Worcestershire sauce
2 × 200g/7oz cans sweetcorn
115g/4oz broad beans (fresh or frozen)
45ml/3 tbsp plain flour
salt and black pepper
fresh parsley sprigs, to garnish

3 Add the chicken pieces and fry until golden brown on all sides, cooking in batches, if necessary. Remove from the pan with tongs and set aside.

4 Reduce the heat and add the onions and peppers to the pan. Cook for 8–10 minutes, until softened.

5 Increase the heat. Add the tomatoes and their juice, the wine, stock or water, parsley and Tabasco sauce and Worcestershire sauce. Stir thoroughly and bring to the boil.

6 Add the chicken to the pan, pushing down into the sauce. Cover, reduce the heat, and simmer for 30 minutes, stirring occasionally.

7 Remove the lid, add the sweetcorn and beans and mix well. Partly cover the pan and cook for 30 minutes.

8 Tilt the pan and skim off as much of the surface fat as possible. Mix the flour with a little water in a small bowl to make a paste.

9 Stir in about 175ml/6fl oz/¾ cup of the hot sauce from the pan into the flour mixture and then stir into the stew and mix well. Cook for 5–8 minutes more, stirring occasionally.

10 Check the seasoning and adjust if necessary. Serve the stew in shallow soup dishes or large bowls, garnished with parsley sprigs.

1 Rinse the chicken pieces under cold water and pat dry with kitchen paper. Sprinkle each piece lightly with salt and a little paprika.

2 Heat the olive oil with the butter in a flameproof casserole or large heavy-based saucepan over a medium-high heat, until the mixture is sizzling and just starting to change colour.

POUSSIN WITH RAISIN STUFFING

INGREDIENTS

Serves 4

250ml/8fl oz/1 cup port
115g/4oz/²/₃ cup raisins
15ml/1 tbsp walnut oil
75g/3oz mushrooms, finely chopped
1 large celery stick, finely chopped
1 small onion, chopped
50g/2oz/1 cup fresh white breadcrumbs
50g/2oz/¹/₂ cup chopped walnuts
15ml/1 tbsp each chopped fresh basil
  and parsley
2.5ml/¹/₂ tsp dried thyme
75g/3oz/6 tbsp butter, melted
4 poussin
salt and black pepper
salad and cherry tomatoes, to serve

1 Preheat the oven to 180°C/350°F/ Gas 4. Place the port and raisins in a bowl and soak for about 20 minutes.

2 Meanwhile, heat the oil in a frying pan. Add the mushrooms, celery, onion and 1.25ml/¼ tsp salt and cook over a low heat for 8–10 minutes, until softened. Leave to cool slightly.

3 Drain the raisins, reserving the port. Combine the raisins, bread-crumbs, walnuts, basil, parsley and thyme in a large bowl. Stir in the mushroom and onion mixture and 50g/2oz/4 tbsp of the butter. Add salt and pepper to taste.

4 Fill the cavity of each poussin with the stuffing mixture. Do not pack down. Tie the legs together, looping the tail with string to enclose the stuffing.

5 Brush each poussin with the remaining butter and place in a baking dish just large enough to hold the birds comfortably. Pour over the reserved port.

6 Roast for about 1 hour, basting occasionally. To test whether they are cooked, pierce the thigh with a skewer: the juices should run clear. Serve accompanied by salad and cherry tomatoes, with the cooking juices poured over each bird.

OVEN-FRIED CHICKEN

Serves 4

4 large chicken portions
50g/2oz/½ cup plain flour
2.5ml/½ tsp salt
1.25ml/¼ tsp black pepper
1 egg
30ml/2 tbsp water
30ml/2 tbsp finely chopped mixed fresh
*   herbs, such as parsley, basil, and*
*   thyme*
115g/4oz/1 cup dried white
*   breadcrumbs*
25g/1oz/¼ cup freshly grated Parmesan
*   cheese*
lemon wedges, to serve

1 Preheat the oven to 200°C/400°F/ Gas 6. Rinse the chicken portions and pat dry with kitchen paper.

2 Combine the flour, salt and pepper on a large plate and stir with a fork to mix. Coat the chicken portions on all sides with the seasoned flour and shake off the excess.

3 Sprinkle a little water on to the chicken portions and coat again lightly with the seasoned flour.

4 Beat the egg with the water in a shallow dish and stir in the herbs. Dip the chicken portions into the egg mixture, turning to coat them evenly.

5 Combine the breadcrumbs and grated Parmesan cheese on a plate. Roll the chicken portions in the breadcrumbs, patting them in with your fingertips to help them stick.

6 Place the chicken portions in a greased shallow tin large enough to hold them in one layer. Bake for 20–30 minutes, until thoroughly cooked and golden brown. To test whether they are cooked, prick with a fork: the juices that run out should be clear, not pink. Serve at once with lemon wedges.

CHICKEN AND MUSHROOM PIE

INGREDIENTS

Serves 6

15g/½oz dried porcini mushrooms
50g/2oz/4 tbsp butter
15g/½oz/2 tbsp plain flour
250ml/8fl oz/1 cup hot chicken stock
50ml/2fl oz/¼ cup single cream
  or milk
1 onion, coarsely chopped
2 carrots, sliced
2 celery sticks, coarsely chopped
50g/2oz fresh mushrooms, quartered
450g/1lb cooked chicken meat, cubed
50g/2oz fresh or frozen peas
salt and black pepper
beaten egg, to glaze

For the pastry
225g/8oz/2 cups plain flour
1.25ml/¼ tsp salt
115g/4oz/½ cup cold butter, cubed
65g/2½oz/⅓ cup white cooking fat,
  cubed
60–120ml/4–8 tablespoons iced water

1 To make the pastry, sift the flour and salt into a bowl. With a pastry blender or two knives, cut in the butter and cooking fat until the mixture resembles breadcrumbs. Sprinkle with 90ml/6 tbsp iced water and mix until the dough holds together. If the dough is too crumbly, add a little more water, 15ml/1 tbsp at a time. Gather the dough into a ball and flatten into a round. Place in a sealed polythene bag and chill for at least 30 minutes.

2 Place the porcini mushrooms in a small bowl. Add hot water to cover and leave to soak for about 30 minutes, until soft. Lift out of the water with a slotted spoon to leave any grit behind and drain on kitchen paper. Discard the soaking water. Preheat the oven to 190°C/375°F/Gas 5.

3 Melt half of the butter in a heavy-based saucepan. Whisk in the flour and cook until bubbling, whisking constantly. Add the warm stock and cook over a medium heat, whisking, until the mixture boils. Cook for 2–3 minutes more, then whisk in the cream or milk. Season with salt and pepper and set aside.

4 Heat the remaining butter in a large non-stick frying pan until sizzling. Add the onion and carrots and cook for about 5 minutes, until softened. Add the celery and fresh mushrooms and cook for a further 5 minutes. Stir in the cooked chicken, peas and drained porcini mushrooms.

5 Add the chicken mixture to the cream sauce and stir to mix. Taste for seasoning. Turn into a 2.5 litre/4 pint rectangular baking dish.

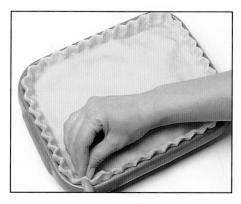

6 Roll out the dough to about a 3mm/⅛in thickness. Cut out a rectangle about 2.5cm/1in larger all around than the dish. Lay the rectangle of dough over the filling. Make a decorative edge by pushing the index finger of one hand between the thumb and index finger of the other.

7 Cut several slits in the pastry to allow steam to escape then brush the pastry with the beaten egg.

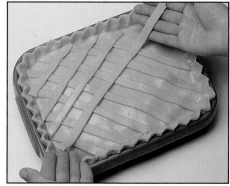

8 Press together the pastry trimmings and roll out again. Cut into thin strips and lay them over the pastry lid. Glaze again. If liked, roll small balls of dough and arrange them in the "windows" in the lattice.

9 Bake for about 30 minutes, until the pastry is browned. Serve the pie hot from the dish.

FISH AND SEAFOOD

Nowadays, supermarkets and fishmongers are positively teeming with different, and often exotic, fish, and this is reflected in this selection of recipes collected from around the world. If you love spicy seafood mixtures, there's a flavourful Italian Fish Stew or Cajun Seafood Gumbo to choose from, while if you prefer your fish less fiery, try Pan-Fried Trout with Tangy Sauce or Fried Fish with Piquant Mayonnaise. Salmon and Prawn Fritters are quick to cook and will appeal to both adults and children – they'd make a delicious party snack too – while if you are cooking for a dinner party you'll find plenty of choice. Prawn Kebabs and Crumb-Coated Prawns are both delicious as a starter, while scallops, cooked either in a flavourful cheese sauce, or with tomatoes to serve with pasta, make excellent special occasion main courses.

PRAWN KEBABS WITH PLUM SAUCE

INGREDIENTS

Serves 6
15ml/1 tbsp vegetable oil
1 onion, finely chopped
1 garlic clove, finely chopped
450g/1lb plums, stoned and chopped
15ml/1 tbsp rice vinegar
30ml/2 tbsp fresh orange juice
5ml/1 tsp Dijon mustard
30ml/2 tbsp soy sauce
15ml/1 tbsp soft light brown sugar
1 point of a star anise
120ml/4fl oz/½ cup water
675g/1½lb raw medium prawns, peeled
(tails left on) and deveined

1 Heat the oil in a saucepan. Add the onion, garlic and plums and cook over a low heat, stirring occasionally for about 10 minutes, until softened.

2 Stir in the vinegar, orange juice, mustard, soy sauce, sugar, star anise and water. Bring to the boil. Lower the heat, cover, and simmer for 20 minutes, stirring occasionally.

3 Uncover the pan and simmer the sauce for 10 minutes more to thicken it, stirring frequently.

4 Remove the star anise. Transfer the sauce to a food processor or blender and purée until smooth.

5 Press the plum sauce through a fine sieve into a saucepan to remove all the fibres and plum skins.

6 Preheat the grill and line the grill pan with foil.

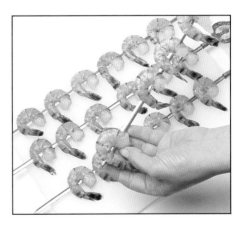

7 Thread the prawns, flat, on to six skewers. Brush them all over with three-quarters of the plum sauce.

8 Place the prawn kebabs in the foil-lined grill pan. Grill for 5–6 minutes, until opaque throughout. Turn the kebabs once.

9 Meanwhile, reheat the remaining plum sauce. Turn into a bowl and serve with the kebabs and rice.

PASTA WITH SCALLOPS IN TOMATO SAUCE

Serves 4

450g/1lb pasta, such as fettucine or
*   linguine*
30ml/2 tbsp olive oil
2 garlic cloves, finely chopped
450g/1lb scallops, sliced in half
*   horizontally*
30ml/2 tbsp chopped fresh basil
salt and black pepper
fresh basil sprigs, to garnish

For the sauce

30ml/2 tbsp olive oil
½ onion, finely chopped
1 garlic clove, finely chopped
salt, to taste
2 × 400g/14oz cans peeled tomatoes

1 To make the sauce, heat the oil in a non-stick frying pan. Add the onion, garlic and a little salt, and cook for about 5 minutes, until just softened, stirring occasionally.

2 Add the tomatoes, with their juice, and crush with a fork. Bring to the boil, then reduce the heat and simmer gently for 15 minutes. Remove the pan from the heat and set aside.

3 Bring a large pan of salted water to the boil. Add the pasta and cook until just tender to the bite, according to instructions on the packet.

4 Meanwhile, combine the oil and garlic in another non-stick frying pan and cook for about 30 seconds, until just sizzling. Add the scallops and 2.5ml/½ tsp salt and cook over a high heat for about 3 minutes, tossing, until the scallops are cooked through.

5 Add the scallops to the tomato sauce. Season with salt and pepper, then stir gently and keep warm.

6 Drain the pasta, rinse under hot water, and drain again. Add the scallop sauce and the basil and toss thoroughly. Serve immediately, garnished with fresh basil sprigs.

SALMON WITH SIZZLING HERBS

INGREDIENTS

Serves 4

4 salmon steaks, 175–200g/6–7oz each
85ml/3fl oz/⅓ cup olive oil
45ml/3 tbsp very finely chopped fresh
  root ginger
50g/2oz/½ cup chopped spring onions
90ml/6 tbsp chopped fresh coriander
60ml/4 tbsp soy sauce, plus extra
  to serve
salt and black pepper

1 Bring some water to the boil in the base of a steamer.

2 Season the salmon steaks on both sides with salt and black pepper.

3 Place the salmon steaks in the top part of the steamer. Cover the pan and steam for 7–8 minutes, until the fish is opaque throughout.

4 Meanwhile, heat the oil in a small heavy-based saucepan until very hot and fry half the ginger and half the spring onions for 30 seconds, stirring all the time.

5 Place the steamed salmon steaks on warmed serving plates.

6 Spoon the chopped fresh coriander over the salmon steaks, then sprinkle with the remaining ginger and spring onions. Drizzle 15ml/1 tbsp of soy sauce over each salmon steak.

7 Spoon the fried ginger, onions and hot oil over each salmon steak and serve at once, with a little extra soy sauce if liked.

Aubergine with Prawn Stuffing

Serves 4

2 large firm aubergines, of equal size
30ml/2 tbsp fresh lemon juice
40g/1½oz/3 tbsp butter or margarine
225g/8oz raw prawns, peeled and
  deveined
50g/2oz spring onions, thinly sliced
350g/12oz fresh tomatoes, deseeded
  and chopped
1 garlic clove, finely chopped
45ml/3 tbsp chopped fresh parsley
45ml/3 tbsp chopped fresh basil
large pinch of grated nutmeg
Tabasco sauce
50g/2oz/½ cup dried white
  breadcrumbs
salt and black pepper
boiled rice, to serve
fresh herbs, to garnish, such as parsley,
  basil and coriander

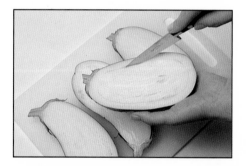

1 Preheat the oven to 190°C/375°F/ Gas 5. Cut the aubergines in half lengthways. Cut around the inside edge of each aubergine half, about 1cm/½in from the skin and carefully scoop out the aubergine flesh.

2 Immerse the aubergine shells, skin side up, in cold water, to prevent them from discolouring.

COOK'S TIP
This can also be served cold as an unusual summer dish.

3 Chop the scooped-out aubergine flesh coarsely, toss with the lemon juice, and set aside.

4 Melt 25g/1oz/2 tbsp of the butter or margarine in a frying pan. Add the prawns and sauté for 2–3 minutes until pink, turning the prawns so they cook evenly. Remove the prawns with a slotted spoon and set aside.

5 Add the spring onions to the frying pan and cook over a medium heat for about 2 minutes, stirring constantly. Add the tomatoes, garlic and parsley and cook for a further 5 minutes.

6 Stir in the chopped aubergines, basil and nutmeg. If necessary, add a little water to prevent the vegetables sticking. Cover and simmer for 8–10 minutes. Remove from the heat.

7 Cut each prawn into two or three pieces. Stir into the vegetable mixture, then season with salt, pepper and Tabasco sauce, to taste.

8 Lightly oil a shallow baking dish large enough to hold the aubergine halves in one layer. Drain and dry the aubergine shells and arrange in the dish.

9 Sprinkle a layer of breadcrumbs into each shell. Spoon in a layer of the prawn mixture. Repeat, finishing with a layer of crumbs.

10 Dot with the remaining butter or margarine. Bake for 20–25 minutes, until bubbling hot and golden brown on top. Serve immediately with rice and garnished with fresh parsley, basil or coriander.

RED SNAPPER WITH CORIANDER SALSA

INGREDIENTS

Serves 4

4 red snapper fillets, about 175g/6oz
  each
22.5ml/1½ tbsp vegetable oil
15g/½oz/1 tbsp butter
salt and black pepper

For the salsa

1 bunch fresh coriander, stalks removed
250ml/8fl oz/1 cup olive oil
2 garlic cloves, chopped
2 tomatoes, seeded and chopped
30ml/2 tbsp fresh orange juice
15ml/1 tbsp sherry vinegar
coriander sprigs and orange peel,
  to garnish
salad, to serve

1 To make the salsa, place the coriander, oil and garlic in a food processor or blender. Process until almost smooth. Add the tomatoes and pulse on and off several times; the mixture should be slightly chunky.

2 Transfer the mixture to a bowl. Stir in the orange juice, vinegar and salt, then set the salsa aside.

3 Rinse the fish fillets and pat dry, then sprinkle on both sides with salt and pepper. Heat the oil and butter in a large frying pan. When hot, add the fish and cook for 2–3 minutes on each side, until opaque throughout. Cook in two batches, if necessary.

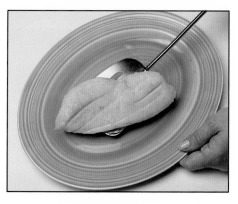

4 Transfer the fillets to warmed serving plates. Top with a spoonful of salsa. Serve garnished with coriander and orange peel.

CRUMB-COATED PRAWNS

INGREDIENTS

Serves 4

90g/3¹/₂oz/³/₄ cup polenta
about 5–10ml/1–2 tsp cayenne
    pepper
2.5ml/¹/₂ tsp ground cumin
5ml/1 tsp salt
30ml/2 tbsp chopped fresh coriander
    or parsley
1kg/2lb raw large prawns, peeled and
    deveined
plain flour, for dredging
45ml/3 tbsp/¹/₄ cup vegetable oil
115g/4oz/1 cup coarsely grated
    Cheddar cheese
lime wedges and fresh tomato salsa,
    to serve

1 Preheat the grill. Mix the polenta, cayenne pepper, cumin, salt and coriander or parsley in a bowl.

2 Coat the prawns lightly in flour, then dip them in water and roll in the polenta mixture to coat evenly.

3 Heat the oil in a frying pan. When hot, add the prawns, in batches if necessary. Cook for 2–3 minutes on each side, until they are cooked through. Drain on kitchen paper.

4 Place the prawns in a large baking dish, or in four individual flameproof dishes. Sprinkle the cheese evenly over the top. Grill for 2–3 minutes, until the cheese melts. Serve immediately, with lime wedges and the tomato salsa.

Cajun Seafood Gumbo

Serves 10–12
1.5kg/3lb raw prawns
1.6 litres/2¾ pints/7 cups water
1 onion, quartered
4 bay leaves
175ml/6fl oz/¾ cup vegetable oil
115g/4oz/1 cup plain flour
50g/2oz/4 tbsp butter or margarine
450g/1lb onions, finely chopped
2 medium green peppers, finely
 chopped
275g/10oz/2 cups finely chopped celery
675g/1½lb spicy Polish or Italian
 sausage, cut into 1cm/½in rounds
450g/1lb fresh okra, cut into
 1cm/½in slices
3 garlic cloves, finely chopped
2.5ml/½ tsp fresh or dried thyme
10ml/2 tsp salt
2.5ml/½ tsp black pepper
2.5ml/½ tsp white pepper
5ml/1 tsp cayenne pepper
few drops of Tabasco sauce (optional)
450g/1lb/2 cups chopped, peeled fresh
 or canned plum tomatoes
450g/1lb fresh crab meat
whole cooked prawns, and bay and
 celery leaves, to garnish
boiled rice, to serve

1 Peel and devein the prawns; reserve the heads and shells. Set the prawns aside in a covered bowl in the fridge while you make the sauce.

2 Put the prawn heads and shells in a saucepan with the water, quartered onion and 1 bay leaf. Bring to the boil, then partly cover and simmer for 20 minutes. Strain and set aside.

3 Heat the oil in a heavy-based, flameproof casserole. When the oil is hot, add the flour, a little at a time, and blend to a smooth paste using a long-handled wooden spoon.

4 Cook over a medium-low heat for 25–40 minutes, stirring constantly, until the roux reaches the desired colour. The roux will gradually deepen in colour from light beige to tan, and then to a deeper, redder brown. When it reaches the colour of pale caramel, remove the pan from the heat and continue stirring until the roux has cooled and stopped cooking.

5 Melt the butter or margarine in a large heavy-based saucepan. Add the onions, green peppers and celery. Cook over a medium-low heat for 6–8 minutes, until the onions are softened, stirring occasionally.

6 Add the sliced sausage and mix well. Cook for 5 minutes more. Stir in the okra and garlic and cook until the okra stops producing white "threads".

7 Add the remaining bay leaves, the thyme, salt, black, white and cayenne peppers, and Tabasco sauce to taste. Mix well. Stir in about 1.5 litres/2½ pints of the prawn stock and the tomatoes. Bring to the boil, then partly cover the pan, lower the heat, and simmer about 20 minutes.

8 Whisk in the roux. Raise the heat and bring to the boil, whisking well. Lower the heat again and simmer, uncovered, for 40–50 minutes more, stirring occasionally.

9 Gently stir in the prawns and crab meat. Cook for 3–4 minutes until the prawns turn pink. Serve the gumbo in deep bowls garnished with a few whole cooked prawns and with bay and celery leaves. Serve hot with boiled rice.

COOK'S TIP
Heavy pans retain their heat. When making a Cajun roux, do not let it get too dark, as the roux will continue cooking off the heat.

PAN-FRIED TROUT WITH TANGY SAUCE

INGREDIENTS

Serves 4
4 rainbow trout, about 175g/6oz each
25g/1oz/¼ cup plain flour
25g/1oz/2 tbsp butter
15ml/1 tbsp vegetable oil
salt and black pepper

For the sauce
120ml/4fl oz/½ cup mayonnaise
120ml/4fl oz/½ cup soured cream
5ml/1 tsp creamed horseradish
1.25ml/¼ tsp paprika
30ml/2 tbsp fresh tomato or
  lemon juice
15ml/1 tbsp chopped fresh herbs, such
  as chives, parsley, or basil
salt and black pepper

1 To make the sauce, place the mayonnaise, soured cream, horseradish, paprika, tomato or lemon juice and herbs in a bowl. Season and mix well, then set aside.

2 Rinse the trout and pat dry. Season the inside of the fish generously with salt and black pepper.

3 Mix the flour, 2.5ml/½ tsp salt and a little black pepper in a shallow dish. Lightly coat the trout on both sides with the seasoned flour, shaking off any excess.

4 Heat the butter and oil in a large non-stick frying pan over a medium-high heat. When sizzling, add the trout and cook for 4–5 minutes on each side, until cooked. Serve at once, with the horseradish mayonnaise.

FRIED FISH WITH PIQUANT MAYONNAISE

Serves 4
1 egg
45ml/3 tbsp olive oil
squeeze of lemon juice
2.5ml/¹⁄₂ tsp finely chopped fresh
  dill or parsley
4 whiting or haddock fillets
50g/2oz/¹⁄₂ cup plain flour
25g/1oz/2 tbsp butter or margarine
salt and black pepper
mixed salad, to serve

For the mayonnaise
1 egg yolk
30ml/2 tbsp Dijon mustard
30ml/2 tbsp white wine vinegar
10ml/2 tsp paprika
300ml/¹⁄₂ pint/1¹⁄₄ cups olive or
  vegetable oil
30ml/2 tbsp creamed horseradish
1 clove garlic, finely chopped
25g/1oz/¹⁄₄ cup finely chopped celery
30ml/2 tbsp tomato ketchup
salt and black pepper

2 When the mixture is smooth and thick, beat in all the other sauce ingredients. Cover the sauce and chill until ready to serve.

4 Dip both sides of each fish fillet in the egg and herb mixture, then coat the fillets lightly and evenly with flour, shaking off the excess.

1 To make the sauce, blend the egg yolk, mustard, vinegar and paprika in a mixing bowl. Add the oil in a thin stream, beating vigorously with a wire whisk to blend it in.

> **VARIATION**
> If preferred, serve the fish fillets with lime or lemon wedges.

3 Combine the egg, 15ml/1 tbsp of the olive oil, the lemon juice, herbs and a little salt and pepper in a shallow dish. Beat until well mixed.

5 Heat the butter or margarine with the remaining olive oil in a large heavy-based frying pan. Fry the fish fillets for 8–10 minutes, until golden brown on both sides and cooked through. If necessary cook the fish in two batches, keeping the cooked fish warm while cooking remainder.

6 Serve the fish hot, with the piquant sauce accompanied by a salad.

SALMON AND PRAWN FRITTERS

Serves 4
½ fennel bulb, cut into pieces
1 medium leek, cut into pieces
1 green pepper, seeded and cut into
    pieces
2 garlic cloves
15g/½oz/1 tbsp butter
large pinch of dried red pepper flakes
175g/6oz skinless boneless salmon,
    cut into pieces
90g/3½oz skinless boneless cod or
    haddock, cut into pieces
75g/3oz cooked prawns, peeled
115g/4oz/1 cup plain flour
6 eggs, beaten
350–475ml/12–16fl oz/1½–2 cups
    milk
15ml/1 tbsp chopped fresh basil
salt and black pepper
60–90ml/4–6 tbsp oil, for greasing
salad leaves and soured cream,
    to serve

1 Place the fennel, leek, pepper and garlic in a food processor and process until finely chopped.

VARIATION
For Salmon and Dill Fritters, increase the amount of salmon to 350 g/12 oz and omit the cod or haddock and prawns. Use dill in place of the basil. Serve with a tossed green salad, if desired.

2 Melt the butter in a frying pan until sizzling. Add the vegetable mixture and red pepper flakes. Season with salt and pepper. Cook for 8–10 minutes over a low heat, until softened. Remove the pan from the heat and set aside.

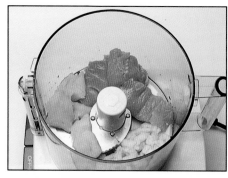

3 Place the salmon and the cod or haddock and prawns in the food processor. Process, using the pulse button and scraping the sides of the bowl several times, until the mixture is coarsely chopped. Transfer to a large bowl and set aside.

4 Sift the flour into a separate bowl and make a well in the centre.

5 Gradually whisk in the eggs alternately with 350ml/12fl oz/1½ cups milk to make a smooth batter. Strain if necessary to remove any lumps.

6 Stir the seafood, vegetables and basil into the batter. If it seems slightly too thick, add a little more milk.

7 Lightly oil a non-stick frying pan or griddle and heat over a medium heat. Drop small spoonfuls of the batter on to the pan and cook for 2–3 minutes, until the fritters are golden around the edges. Turn them over and cook the other side for 2–3 minutes more. Work in batches, keeping the cooked fritters warm. Serve hot, with salad leaves and spoonfuls of soured cream.

SCALLOPS THERMIDOR

INGREDIENTS

Serves 6

1kg/2lb scallops
50g/2oz/½ cup plain flour
115g/4oz/½ cup butter or margarine
50g/2oz/1 cup small mushrooms,
  quartered
25g/1oz/½ cup fresh white
  breadcrumbs
30ml/2 tbsp finely chopped
  fresh parsley
30ml/2 tbsp snipped fresh chives
120ml/4fl oz/½ cup sherry
45ml/3 tbsp brandy
5ml/1 tsp Worcestershire sauce
2.5ml/½ tsp salt
1.25ml/¼ tsp black pepper
350ml/12fl oz/1½ cups single cream
2 egg yolks
chives, to garnish

1 Roll the scallops in the flour. Heat half the butter or margarine in a frying pan. Shake off the excess flour, then sauté the scallops in the pan for 3 minutes, until just golden. Remove from the pan and set aside. Preheat the oven to 200°C/400°F/Gas 6.

2 Melt 25g/1oz/2 tbsp of the remaining butter or margarine in the pan. Add the mushrooms and breadcrumbs and sauté over a medium heat for 3–4 minutes, stirring. Add the herbs, sherry, brandy, Worcestershire sauce, salt and pepper and cook for a further 3–4 minutes, stirring well.

3 Add the cream and cook over a low heat for another 3–4 minutes, stirring occasionally. Remove the pan from the heat and mix in the egg yolks. Stir in the sautéed scallops.

4 Divide the mixture among six buttered individual gratin or other baking dishes. Or, if you prefer, turn the mixture into one large shallow baking dish. Dot with the remaining butter or margarine.

5 Bake for about 10 minutes, until bubbling and browned. Serve immediately garnished with chives tied into bundles with another chive.

ITALIAN FISH STEW

INGREDIENTS

Serves 4
30ml/2 tbsp olive oil
1 onion, thinly sliced
a few saffron threads
5ml/1 tsp dried thyme
large pinch of cayenne pepper
2 garlic cloves, finely chopped
2 × 400g/14oz cans peeled tomatoes,
    drained and chopped
175ml/6fl oz/³⁄₄ cup dry white wine
1.85 litres/3¼ pints/8 cups hot fish
    stock
350g/12oz white, skinless fish fillets,
    cut into pieces
450g/1lb monkfish, membrane
    removed, cut into pieces
450g/1lb mussels in the shell,
    thoroughly scrubbed
225g/8oz small squid, cleaned and cut
    into rings
30ml/2 tbsp chopped fresh basil
    or parsley
salt and black pepper
thickly sliced bread, to serve

1 Heat the oil in a large, heavy-based saucepan. Add the onion, saffron, thyme, cayenne pepper and salt, to taste. Stir well and cook over a low heat for 8–10 minutes, until soft. Add the garlic and cook for a further 1 minute.

COOK'S TIP
Choose firm white fish fillets, such as cod, haddock, huss or hoki, which will hold their shape.

2 Stir in the tomatoes, wine and fish stock. Bring to the boil and boil for 1 minute, then reduce the heat and simmer gently for 15 minutes.

3 Add the fish fillet and monkfish pieces to the pan and simmer gently for a further 3 minutes.

4 Add the mussels and squid and simmer for about 2 minutes, until the mussels open. Stir in the basil or parsley and season to taste.

5 Ladle into warmed soup bowls and serve immediately, with bread.

BAKED HADDOCK WITH TOMATOES

INGREDIENTS

Serves 6

1kg/2¼lb thick haddock fillets,
skinned
45ml/3 tbsp olive oil
5ml/1 tsp drained capers, chopped
2 garlic cloves, chopped
2 ripe tomatoes, peeled, seeded, and
finely diced
30ml/2 tbsp chopped fresh basil
250ml/8fl oz/1 cup dry white wine
salt and black pepper
sprigs of basil, to garnish
salad leaves, to serve

1 Preheat the oven to 200°C/400°F/
Gas 6. Arrange the fillets in an
oiled baking dish. Brush with oil.

2 Mix together the capers, garlic,
tomatoes and basil. Season well.

3 Spoon the tomato mixture over the
fish and pour in the wine. Bake for
15–20 minutes, until the fish is cooked
and opaque in the centre. Garnish each
serving with sprigs of basil and serve
with salad leaves.

LEMON SOLE WITH CRAB

INGREDIENTS

Serves 6

50g/2oz/4 tbsp butter or margarine
45ml/3 tbsp plain flour
250ml/8fl oz/1 cup fish stock, or 175ml/
6fl oz/¾ cup fish stock mixed with
45ml/3 tbsp dry white wine
250ml/8fl oz/1 cup milk
1 bay leaf
6 lemon sole fillets, halved lengthways
200g/7oz can crab meat, drained
90ml/6 tbsp freshly grated
Parmesan cheese
salt and black pepper
flat leaf parsley, to garnish
cherry tomatoes and lettuce leaves,
to serve

1 Preheat the oven to 220°C/425°F/
Gas 7 and butter a large shallow
baking dish.

> **VARIATIONS**
> Other flat white fish, such as
> plaice, can be substituted for the
> lemon sole, if you prefer.

2 Melt the butter or margarine in a
medium-sized, heavy-based
saucepan over a medium heat. Stir in
the flour and cook for 2–3 minutes.

3 Pour in the fish stock (or the mixed
fish stock and wine) together with
the milk and whisk until smooth.

4 Add the bay leaf. Raise the heat to
high and bring to the boil. Cook for
3–4 minutes. Then remove the sauce
from the heat and add salt to taste.
Keep warm while preparing the fish.

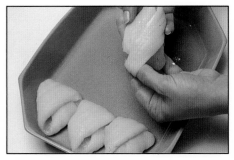

5 Twist each fish fillet to form a neat
cone shape and arrange in the
prepared baking dish. Sprinkle the crab
meat over the fish. Pour the hot sauce
evenly over the top and sprinkle with
the Parmesan cheese.

6 Bake for 10–12 minutes, until the
top is golden brown and the fish is
cooked. Serve garnished with flat leaf
parsley and accompanied by cherry
tomatoes and lettuce leaves.

VEGETABLE DISHES AND SALADS

Even if you are not vegetarian, you will find recipes to tempt you in this superb selection. There's a fantastic Vegetable Chilli to serve with baked potatoes for an informal dinner; Cheesy Courgette Casserole; Macaroni and Blue Cheese; and a delicious Deep-Pan Pizza; all of which are ideal for mid-week family meals. There's also an aromatic Onion and Thyme Tart to serve hot or cold with salad for a week-end meal. There are salads, too: Warm Rocket Salad with Bacon would be delicious served as a starter on a special occasion, while one of the bean salads featured here would make a filling lunch on its own, and either could be served as an accompaniment to grilled meat, poultry or fish. Other vegetable side dishes include Fried Tomatoes in Cream, Carrot and Parsnip Mash, and Sweetcorn with Peppers.

VEGETABLE CHILLI

Serves 8

*45ml/3 tbsp extra virgin olive or
   vegetable oil
2 onions, chopped
2 celery sticks, finely sliced
2 carrots, cut into 1cm/½in cubes
2 garlic cloves, finely chopped
2.5ml/½ tsp celery seeds
2.5ml/¼ tsp cayenne pepper
5ml/1 tsp ground cumin
15–45ml/1–3 tbsp chilli powder,
   to taste
2 × 400g/14oz cans chopped tomatoes
   with their juice
250ml/8fl oz/1 cup vegetable stock
   or water
7.5ml/1½ tsp salt
2.5ml/½ tsp fresh or dried thyme
1 bay leaf
115g/4oz cauliflower florets
3–4 medium courgettes, cut into
   1cm/½in cubes
115g/4oz frozen or canned sweetcorn
400g/14oz can kidney beans, drained
Tabasco sauce (optional)*

2 Stir in the celery seeds, cayenne pepper, cumin and chilli powder. Add the tomatoes, stock or water, salt, thyme and bay leaf then stir well and cook for 15 minutes, uncovered.

3 Add the cauliflower, courgettes and sweetcorn. Cover the casserole or pan and cook for a further 15 minutes.

4 Add the kidney beans, stir well and cook for a further 10 minutes, uncovered. Check the seasoning, and add a dash of Tabasco sauce if liked. Serve piping hot with boiled rice, noodles or baked potatoes.

1 Heat the oil in a large flameproof casserole or heavy-based saucepan and add the onions, celery, carrots and garlic. Cover the casserole and cook over a low heat for 8–10 minutes, stirring from time to time, until the onions are softened.

Boston Baked Beans

INGREDIENTS

Serves 8

675g/1½lb/3 cups dried navy or
    soya beans
1 bay leaf
4 cloves
2 onions
175g/6oz molasses or black treacle
165g/5½oz/¾ cup soft dark brown
    sugar
15ml/1 tbsp Dijon mustard
5ml/1 tsp salt
5ml/1 tsp black pepper
250ml/8fl oz/1 cup boiling water
225g/8oz piece salt pork

1 Rinse the beans under cold running water. Drain and place in a large bowl. Cover with cold water and leave to soak overnight.

2 Drain and rinse the beans. Put them in a large pan with the bay leaf and cover with fresh cold water. Bring to the boil and boil rapidly for 10 minutes. Reduce the heat and simmer for 1½–2 hours, until tender. Drain. Preheat the oven to 140°C/275°F/Gas 1.

3 Put the beans in a large casserole. Stick two cloves in each of the onions and add them to the casserole.

4 Place the molasses or treacle, dark brown sugar, mustard, salt and pepper in a mixing bowl. Add the boiling water and stir to blend.

5 Pour this mixture over the beans. Add more water if necessary so the beans are almost covered with liquid.

6 Blanch the piece of salt pork in boiling water for 3 minutes. Drain. Score the rind with deep cuts 1cm/½in apart. Add the salt pork to the casserole and push down just below the surface of the beans, skin-side up.

7 Cover the casserole and bake in the centre of the oven for 4½–5 hours. Uncover for the last 30 minutes, so the pork rind becomes brown and crisp. Slice or shred the pork and serve hot.

Sweet and Sour Beetroot

INGREDIENTS

Serves 6

5 medium cooked beetroot (about
    675g/1½lb)
50g/2oz/⅓ cup caster sugar
15ml/1 tbsp cornflour
2.5ml/½ tsp salt
50ml/2fl oz/¼ cup cider or white wine
    vinegar
120ml/4fl oz/½ cup beetroot cooking
    liquid or water
25g/1oz/2 tbsp butter or margarine
fresh parsley sprig, to garnish

1 Peel the beetroot and cut them into thick slices. Set aside.

2 Place the sugar, cornflour, salt, vinegar and beetroot liquid or water in the top of a double boiler and stir until smooth. Cook over a pan of hot water, stirring constantly, until the mixture is smooth.

3 Add the beetroot and butter or margarine. Cook over the hot water for about 10 minutes, stirring occasionally, until the beetroot is hot. Serve garnished with a parsley sprig.

ONION AND THYME TART

INGREDIENTS

Serves 6

*25g/1oz/2 tbsp butter or 30ml/2 tbsp
   olive oil*
275g/10oz onions, thinly sliced
2.5ml/½ tsp fresh or dried thyme leaves
1 egg
*120ml/4fl oz/½ cup soured cream or
   natural yogurt*
10ml/2 tsp poppy seeds
1.25ml/¼ tsp ground mace or nutmeg
salt and black pepper

For the pastry base

115g/4oz/1 cup plain flour
6.25ml/1¼ tsp baking powder
2.5ml/½ tsp salt
*40g/1½oz/3 tbsp cold butter or white
   cooking fat*
90ml/6 tbsp milk

1 Heat the butter or oil in a medium-sized frying pan. Add the onions and cook over a low heat for 10–12 minutes until soft and golden. Add the thyme and season with salt and pepper. Remove the pan from the heat and leave to cool. Preheat the oven to 220°C/425°F/Gas 7.

2 To make the pastry base, sift the flour, baking powder and salt into a bowl. Dice the butter or cooking fat, add to the dry ingredients and rub in with your fingertips. Add the milk and stir in lightly with a wooden spoon to make a soft dough.

3 Turn out the dough on to a floured work surface and knead lightly until smooth.

4 Lightly grease a 20cm/8in baking tin that is at least 5cm/2in deep. Pat out the dough into a round of the same size and press it into the base of the tin. Cover with the onions.

5 Beat together the egg and soured cream or yogurt and spread evenly over the onions. Sprinkle with the poppy seeds and mace or nutmeg. Bake for 25–30 minutes, until the egg topping is puffed and golden.

6 Leave to cool in the tin for 10 minutes. Slip a knife between the tart and the tin to loosen, then unmould on to a plate. Cut the tart into wedges and serve warm.

POTATO AND CHEESE TORTILLA

INGREDIENTS

Serves 4

15ml/1 tbsp vegetable oil
½ onion, sliced
1 small green pepper, seeded and cut
  into rings
1 garlic clove, finely chopped
1 tomato, chopped
6 stoned black olives, chopped
275g/10oz potatoes, cooked
  and sliced
50g/2oz sliced chorizo, cut
  into strips
fresh green chilli, seeded and
  chopped
50g/2oz/½ cup grated Cheddar cheese
6 size 1 eggs
45ml/3 tbsp milk
1.25ml/¼ tsp ground cumin
1.25ml/¼ tsp dried oregano
1.25ml/¼ tsp paprika
salt and black pepper

1 Preheat the oven to 190°C/375°F/ Gas 5. Lightly grease a 23cm/9in round cake tin.

2 Heat the oil in a non-stick frying pan. Add the onion, pepper and garlic and cook over a medium heat for 5–8 minutes, until softened.

3 Turn the vegetables into the prepared tin. Add the chopped tomato, olives, potatoes, chorizo and chilli. Sprinkle with the grated cheese and set aside.

4 Place the eggs and milk in a bowl and whisk until frothy. Add the cumin, oregano, paprika and salt and pepper to taste. Whisk to blend.

5 Pour the egg mixture on to the vegetables, tilting the tin so that the egg mixture spreads evenly.

6 Bake for 30 minutes, until set and lightly golden. Serve hot or cold.

COLESLAW WITH CARAWAY

INGREDIENTS

Serves 8

250ml/8fl oz/1 cup mayonnaise
120ml/4fl oz/½ cup white
   wine vinegar
15ml/1 tbsp Dijon mustard
10ml/2 tsp caster sugar
15ml/1 tbsp caraway seeds
1 white cabbage, finely sliced
2 carrots, grated
1 small onion, finely sliced
salt and black pepper
fresh parsley sprigs, to garnish

1 Mix together the mayonnaise, vinegar, mustard, sugar and caraway seeds. Season well.

2 Place the cabbage, carrots and sliced onions in a large bowl.

3 Add the dressing to the vegetables and mix well. Taste for seasoning, then cover and chill for about 1–2 hours. Stir the coleslaw and serve garnished with parsley sprigs.

FRIED TOMATOES WITH CREAM

INGREDIENTS

Serves 4

225g/8oz large firm red tomatoes
40g/1½oz/3 tbsp plain flour
50g/2oz/4 tbsp butter or bacon dripping
sugar, to taste
4 slices hot buttered toast
175ml/6fl oz/¾ cup single cream
salt and black pepper
fresh parsley sprigs, to garnish

1 Slice the tomatoes into 1cm/½in rounds and coat lightly with flour.

2 Heat the butter or bacon fat in a frying pan. When it is hot, add the tomato slices and cook until browned. Turn them once, and season generously with salt and pepper.

3 If the tomatoes are green, sprinkle each slice with a little sugar. Cook for a further 3–4 minutes, until the other side is well browned.

4 Divide the tomatoes among the slices of toast and keep hot.

5 Pour the cream into the hot frying pan and bring to simmering point. Cook for 1–2 minutes, stirring to mix in the cooking juices. Spoon the sauce over the tomatoes, and serve immediately garnished with parsley.

> **VARIATION**
> To make Fried Tomatoes with Ham, top the toast with ham slices before covering with the tomatoes.

CARROT AND PARSNIP MASH

Serves 6
450g/1lb parsnips, cut into 1cm/¹/₂in
  slices
450g/1lb carrots, cut into 1cm/¹/₂in
  slices
65g/2¹/₂oz/¹/₂ cup chopped onion
1 bay leaf
10ml/2 tsp granulated sugar
1.25ml/¹/₄ tsp salt
250ml/8fl oz/1 cup water
25g/1oz/2 tbsp butter or 30ml/2 tbsp
  olive oil
fresh snipped chives, to garnish

1 Put the parsnip and carrot slices in a medium-sized saucepan with the chopped onion, bay leaf, sugar and salt. Pour on the water.

2 Cover the pan tightly and cook over a medium heat for about 20 minutes, stirring occasionally, until the vegetables are just tender. Check from time to time to make sure the water has not evaporated, and add a little more if necessary.

3 Drain most of the water from the vegetables and discard the bay leaf. Purée the vegetables in a food processor or food mill. Beat in the butter or olive oil and turn into a warmed serving dish. Sprinkle with the snipped chives and serve immediately.

BAKED SQUASH WITH HERBS

Serves 4
2 medium acorn squash
90ml/6 tbsp finely chopped mixed fresh
  chives, thyme, basil, and parsley
50g/2oz/4 tbsp butter or margarine
salt and black pepper
fresh leaves, to garnish

1 Cut each squash in half horizontally and scoop out the seeds and stringy fibres. If necessary, cut a small slice off the base of each squash half so that it sits squarely.

2 Preheat the oven to 190°C/375°F/ Gas 5. Spoon one-quarter of the mixed chopped herbs into the hollows of each squash half.

> **VARIATION**
> For Caramel-Baked Squash,
> replace the herbs with 50g/4 tbsp
> dark brown sugar. Melt the butter
> or margarine, dissolve the brown
> sugar in it and fill the squashes.

3 Top each squash half with 15g/ ¹/₂oz/1 tbsp butter or margarine and season with salt and pepper.

4 Arrange the four squash halves in a shallow baking dish large enough to hold them in one layer. Pour boiling water into the dish, to a depth of about 2.5cm/1in. Cover the dish loosely with a piece of foil.

5 Bake for 45–60 minutes, until the squash is tender when pierced. Serve hot, garnished with fresh herbs.

Cheesy Courgette Casserole

Ingredients

Serves 4

1 garlic clove, bruised
30ml/2 tbsp olive oil or melted
  butter
1kg/2lb courgettes
225g/8oz/2 cups coarsely grated
  Cheddar cheese
2 eggs
350ml/12fl oz/1½ cups milk
salt and black pepper
fresh parsley sprigs, to garnish

Variation
For a spicier version, toss the
sliced courgettes with 5–10ml/
1–2 tsp chilli powder.

1 Preheat the oven to 190°C/375°F/
Gas 5. Rub the garlic clove around
the inside of an ovenproof dish,
pressing hard to extract the juice;
discard the garlic clove. Grease the dish
lightly with a little of the olive oil or
melted butter.

2 Cut the courgettes into 5mm/¼in
slices. Place them in a bowl and
toss with the remaining oil or melted
butter. Add salt to taste.

3 Arrange half the courgette slices in
an even layer in the baking dish.
Sprinkle with half the cheese. Add the
remaining courgette slices, spreading
them evenly on top.

4 Place the eggs, milk with a little salt
and pepper to taste in a measuring
jug and whisk together. Pour over the
courgettes and sprinkle with the
remaining cheese.

5 Cover with foil and bake for about
30 minutes. Remove the foil and
bake for a further 30–40 minutes more,
until the top is browned. Serve hot,
warm, or cold, garnished with parsley.

THREE BEAN AND LENTIL SALAD

INGREDIENTS

Serves 6

*175g/6oz dried chick peas, soaked
overnight in water and drained*
*175g/6oz dried red kidney beans,
soaked overnight in water and
drained*
3 bay leaves
*90g/3½oz/½ cup green or brown
lentils*
*225g/8oz green beans, cut into 2.5cm/
1in slices and cooked*
1 small onion, finely chopped
3 spring onions, chopped
15ml/1 tbsp chopped fresh parsley

For the dressing

*75–90ml/5–6 tbsp red wine
vinegar*
10ml/2 tsp Dijon mustard
90ml/6 tbsp olive oil
1 garlic clove, crushed
coarse salt and black pepper

3 When the chick peas and beans are nearly ready put the lentils in a large pan and add cold water to cover and the remaining bay leaf. Bring to the boil, then cover and simmer for 30–40 minutes, until just tender.

4 As the lentils, beans and chick peas finish cooking, drain them thoroughly in a colander and transfer them to a large mixing bowl. Discard the bay leaves.

5 Add the green beans, red onion, spring onions and parsley to the bowl. Add the dressing and toss well.

6 Taste the salad and adjust the seasoning, adding more vinegar and salt and pepper if necessary. Serve at room temperature.

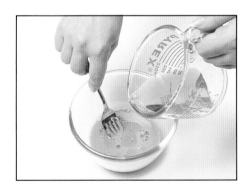

1 To make the dressing, in a bowl mix 60ml/4 tbsp of the vinegar and the salt with a fork until dissolved, then stir in the mustard. Gradually stir in the oil until blended. Add the garlic and pepper to taste and set aside.

2 Put the chick peas and kidney beans in separate large pans. Add a bay leaf to each and cover with cold water. Bring to the boil and boil for 10 minutes, then cover and simmer for 30 minutes. Add salt, to taste, to each pan and continue simmering for ½–1½ hours, until tender.

Chicago Deep-Pan Pizza

INGREDIENTS

Serves 4–6

450g/1lb/4 cups strong plain flour
5ml/1 tsp salt
1 sachet easy-blend dry yeast
45ml/3 tbsp olive oil
250ml/8fl oz/1 cup lukewarm water

For the topping
45ml/3 tbsp olive oil
225g/8oz mozzarella cheese, diced
425g/15oz can chopped tomatoes
50g/2oz freshly grated Parmesan
   cheese
salt and black pepper
handful of fresh basil leaves,
   to garnish

1 Put the flour in a food processor fitted with the dough blade. Add the salt, easy-blend yeast, olive oil and warm water. Process until the dough begins to form a ball. If the dough is too sticky, add a little more flour. If it will not mass together, add a little more warm water and process again.

2 Turn out the dough on to a lightly floured surface and knead for about 5 minutes, until smooth and elastic. Alternatively, process dough in food processor for 1 minute.

3 Form the dough into a ball and place in a lightly oiled large bowl. Cover with clear film and leave to rise in a warm place for about 1½ hours until the dough almost doubles in size. Preheat the oven to 230°C/450°F/Gas 8.

4 Punch down the dough and knead it lightly for 2–3 minutes. Place in a deep, oiled 23–25cm/9–10in pizza tin. Using your fingertips, stretch and pat out the dough thinly so that it lines the tin evenly and neatly.

5 Prick the dough evenly all over with a fork. Bake for 5 minutes.

6 Brush the pizza dough base with 15ml/1 tbsp of olive oil. Sprinkle with the mozzarella, leaving the rim clear. Spoon the tomatoes over the mozzarella and sprinkle with the Parmesan cheese. Season, and drizzle over the remaining olive oil.

7 Bake for 25–30 minutes, until the crust is golden brown and the topping is bubbling hot. Scatter over the basil leaves and serve hot.

MACARONI AND BLUE CHEESE

INGREDIENTS

Serves 6
450g/1lb macaroni
1.2 litres/2 pints/5 cups milk
50g/2oz/4 tbsp butter
75g/3oz plain flour
225g/8oz blue Stilton cheese,
  crumbled
salt and black pepper

1 Preheat the oven to 180°C/350°F/
Gas 4. Grease a shallow
33 × 23cm/13 × 9in ovenproof dish.

2 Bring a large pan of salted water to
the boil. Add the macaroni and
cook for 10–12 minutes, until just
tender. Drain the macaroni and rinse
under cold running water. Place in a
large bowl. Set aside.

3 In another pan, bring the milk to
the boil and set aside.

4 Melt the butter in a heavy-based
saucepan over a low heat. Whisk in
the flour and cook for 1–2 minutes,
whisking constantly and taking care not
to let the mixture brown.

5 Remove the pan from the heat and
whisk the hot milk into the butter
and flour mixture. When the mixture is
smoothly blended, return to a medium
heat and continue cooking, whisking
constantly for about 5 minutes, until
the sauce is thick. Season to taste.

6 Stir the sauce into the macaroni.
Add three-quarters of the crumbled
blue cheese and stir well. Transfer the
macaroni mixture to the prepared
ovenproof dish and spread evenly.

7 Sprinkle the remaining cheese
evenly over the surface. Bake for
about 25 minutes, until the macaroni is
bubbling hot.

8 Preheat the grill and lightly brown
the top of the macaroni and cheese.
Serve immediately, sprinkled with extra
freshly ground black pepper, if you like.

SWEETCORN WITH PEPPERS

── INGREDIENTS ──

Serves 4

30ml/2 tbsp peanut or olive oil
½ onion, finely chopped
2 celery sticks, finely chopped
½ small red pepper, finely chopped
3 × 200g/7oz cans sweetcorn,
*   drained*
2.5ml/½ tsp cayenne pepper
120ml/4fl oz/½ cup dry white wine
*   or water*
1 tomato, seeded and diced
45ml/3 tbsp single cream
30ml/2 tbsp shredded fresh
*   basil leaves*
salt and black pepper
fresh basil sprig, to garnish

1 Heat the oil in a heavy-based saucepan or frying pan. Add the onion and cook over a low heat for 8–10 minutes, until softened, stirring occasionally.

2 Increase the heat slightly, add the celery and red pepper and cook for a further 5 minutes, stirring.

3 Stir in the sweetcorn and the cayenne pepper and cook for about 10 minutes, until the sweetcorn begins to stick to the base of the pan.

4 Pour in the wine or water and scrape up the sweetcorn from the base of the pan. Add the tomato and salt and pepper. Mix well. Cover and cook over a low heat for 8–10 minutes, until the tomato has softened.

5 Stir in the cream and basil and serve, garnished with a basil sprig.

CABBAGE AND RICE

── INGREDIENTS ──

Serves 4

475ml/16fl oz/2 cups chicken or
*   meat stock*
200g/7oz/1 cup long grain rice
15g/½oz/1 tbsp butter or margarine
450g/1lb cabbage or spring greens,
*   chopped*
salt and black pepper

1 Bring the stock to a boil in a large saucepan. Stir in the rice, butter or margarine and salt.

2 Add the cabbage or spring greens, a handful at a time, stirring well after each addition. Bring back to the boil, then cover tightly, reduce the heat, and cook for 15–20 minutes, or until the rice is tender. Season with pepper before serving.

Warm Rocket Salad with Bacon

INGREDIENTS

Serves 6

*115g/4oz rocket or baby spinach
  leaves*
1 Little Gem lettuce
4 spring onions, thinly sliced
*8 back bacon rashers, cut across into
  thin strips*
45ml/3 tbsp fresh lemon juice
10ml/2 tsp caster sugar
5ml/1 tsp Dijon mustard
salt and black pepper

1 Carefully pick over the rocket or baby spinach leaves and wash thoroughly in several changes of water, discarding any thick stalks. Pat dry. Wash and dry the lettuce leaves.

2 Tear each salad leaf into two or three pieces. Arrange a mixture of leaves on individual serving plates and sprinkle with the sliced spring onions.

3 Cook the bacon strips in a small frying pan, until crisp. Remove the bacon with a slotted spoon and drain on kitchen paper.

4 Add the lemon juice, sugar and mustard to the bacon fat in the pan. Heat the mixture gently for 3–4 minutes, scraping up the browned bits in the cooking juices and blending in the mustard with a wooden spoon.

5 Spoon the hot dressing over the salad and sprinkle with the bacon strips and freshly ground black pepper, if you like. Serve at once.

COOK'S TIP
Rocket, which has a delicious, peppery flavour, is becoming increasingly available in large supermarkets and good green-grocers. You can also often buy mixed bags of rocket and other salad leaves, which would be ideal to use in this salad.

WARM SALAD OF BLACK-EYE BEANS

INGREDIENTS

Serves 4

2 small red peppers
2.5ml/½ tsp Dijon mustard
30ml/2 tbsp red wine vinegar
90ml/6 tbsp olive oil
30ml/2 tbsp snipped fresh chives
2 × 425g/15oz cans black-eye beans
1 bay leaf
8 rashers bacon
salt and black pepper
fresh parsley sprig, to garnish

3 Mix together the mustard and vinegar in a small bowl. Add salt and pepper, then beat in the oil until well blended. Add the chives.

5 Drain the black-eye beans in a colander and discard the bay leaf. Tip the beans into a large bowl and, while they are still warm, toss them with the chive dressing.

4 Place the black-eye beans, their liquid and the bay leaf in a large saucepan. Simmer for 3–5 minutes, until warmed through. Meanwhile, grill or fry the bacon until crisp. Drain the bacon on kitchen paper, then cut or break into small pieces.

6 Spoon the beans into a serving dish. Sprinkle with the reserved bacon pieces and scatter over the strips of red pepper. Serve warm, garnished with a sprig of parsley.

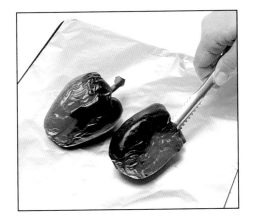

1 Preheat the grill. Grill the peppers until the skin blackens and blisters, turning the peppers so that all sides are charred. Remove from the grill and place in a plastic bag to steam. Leave to cool for 10 minutes.

2 Peel off the skins. Cut the peppers in half, discard the seeds, white membranes, and stem, and slice into thick strips. Set aside.

COOK'S TIP
If preferred, chop the roasted red peppers rather than cutting them into strips and mix into the warm beans with the dressing.

HOT PUDDINGS AND PIES

Warming pies and tarts make a wonderful finish to any meal throughout the year. In cooler weather, choose autumn and winter fruits to make an old-fashioned Blackberry Cobbler, or crispy-topped Apple Brown Betty. Or, instead of fruit, opt for a different sweet filling – there's a butterscotch-flavoured Brown Sugar Pie; the American favourite, Peanut Butter Tart; and a delicious Cider Pie to choose from. In summer, use home-grown seasonal fruits to make open tarts; delicious double crust pies; or a simple, yet scrumptious, Rhubarb and Strawberry Crumble. When fresh ripe peaches are available, bake them in the oven to serve warm with a tangy raspberry sauce. If you are cooking for children there are plenty of appealing recipes, but crisp Apple Fritters will be especially popular.

BAKED BLUEBERRY PUDDING

INGREDIENTS

Serves 10

225g/8oz/2 cups plain flour
15ml/1 tbsp baking powder
pinch of salt
65g/2½oz/⅓ cup butter or margarine,
    at room temperature
150g/5oz/¾ cup caster sugar
1 egg
250ml/8fl oz/1 cup milk
2.5ml/½ tsp grated lemon rind
225g/8oz blueberries
115g/4oz/1 cup icing sugar
30ml/2 tbsps fresh lemon juice
cream or ice cream, to serve

1 Preheat the oven to 180°C/350°F/ Gas 4. Grease a large baking dish.

2 Sift together the flour, baking powder and salt into a bowl.

3 Beat the butter or margarine with the caster sugar in a large bowl, until light and fluffy. Beat in the egg and milk, then fold in the flour mixture, mixing well until evenly blended. Stir in the lemon rind.

4 Spread half of the mixture in the prepared baking dish. Sprinkle with half the blueberries. Top with the remaining mixture and sprinkle with the rest of the blueberries. Bake for 35–45 minutes, until golden brown and a skewer inserted in the centre comes out clean.

5 Mix the icing sugar gradually into the lemon juice to make a smooth icing of pourable consistency. Drizzle the icing over the top of the warm pudding. Serve the pudding warm with cream or ice cream.

Apple Fritters

Serves 4–6
165g/5½oz/1⅓ cups plain flour
10ml/2 tsp baking powder
pinch of salt
150ml/¼ pint/⅔ cup milk
1 egg, beaten
oil, for deep-frying
150g/5oz/¾ cup caster sugar
5ml/1 tsp ground cinnamon
2 large tart cooking apples, peeled,
cored, and cut into 5mm/¼in
thick slices
icing sugar, for dusting

1 Sift the flour, baking powder and salt into a bowl. Beat in the milk and egg with a wire whisk to make a smooth batter.

2 Heat 7.5cm/3in of oil in a heavy-based frying pan to 182°C/360°F.

3 Mix together the caster sugar and cinnamon in a shallow bowl or plate. Toss the apple slices in the sugar mixture to coat all over.

4 Dip the apple slices in the batter, using a fork or slotted spoon. Drain off the excess batter. Fry, in batches, in the hot oil for about 4–5 minutes, until golden brown on both sides. Drain the fritters on kitchen paper.

5 Sprinkle the fritters with icing sugar and serve hot.

Cherry Compôte

Serves 6
120ml/4fl oz/½ cup water
120ml/4fl oz/½ cup red wine
50g/2oz/¼ cup soft light brown sugar
40g/1½oz/¼ cup caster sugar
15ml/1 tbsp honey
2 × 2.5cm/1in strips orange rind
1.25ml/¼ tsp almond essence
675g/1½lb fresh cherries, stoned
strips of orange rind, to decorate
ice cream or whipped cream, to serve

> **VARIATION**
> Fresh, ripe plums may be used for the compôte instead of cherries. Halve and stone them, then add to the sauce in step 2.

1 Combine all the ingredients except the cherries in a large pan. Stir over a medium heat until the sugar dissolves, then increase the heat and boil until the liquid reduces slightly.

2 Add the cherries. Bring back to the boil. Reduce the heat slightly and simmer for 8–10 minutes. If necessary, skim off any foam.

3 Leave to cool to lukewarm, then spoon warm over vanilla ice cream, or chill and serve cold with whipped cream, if you prefer.

Pear and Cherry Crunch

Serves 6

1kg/2¼lb pears (about 8)
45ml/3 tbsp lemon juice
175g/6oz/3 cups fresh white
  breadcrumbs
75g/3oz/6 tbsp butter, melted
75g/3oz/⅔ cup dried cherries or stoned
  prunes, chopped
65g/2½oz/⅔ cup coarsely chopped
  hazelnuts
115g/4oz/½ cup soft light brown sugar
15–25g/½–1oz/1–2 tablespoons butter,
  cut into small pieces
fresh mint sprigs, to decorate
whipped cream, to serve

1 Preheat the oven to 190°C/375°F/ Gas 5. Grease a 20cm/8in square cake tin. Peel, core and chop the pears. Place them in a bowl and sprinkle them with the lemon juice to prevent discolouration.

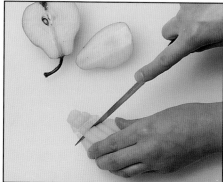

2 Mix together the breadcrumbs and melted butter in a bowl. Spread a scant one-third of the crumb mixture on the bottom of the prepared tin.

3 Top with half the pears. Sprinkle over half the dried cherries or prunes, half the hazelnuts and half the sugar. Repeat the layers, then finish with a layer of crumbs.

4 Dot with the pieces of butter. Bake for 30–35 minutes, until golden. Serve hot, with whipped cream and decorated with a sprig of fresh mint.

BAKED APPLE DUMPLINGS

INGREDIENTS

Serves 8

500g/1lb 2oz/4¹/₂ cups plain flour
2.5ml/¹/₂ tsp salt
350g/12oz/1¹/₂ cups butter or white
  cooking fat
175–250ml/6–8fl oz/³/₄–1 cup
  iced water
8 firm cooking apples
1 egg white
130g/4¹/₂oz/²/₃ cup caster sugar
45ml/3 tbsp whipping cream
2.5ml/¹/₂ tsp vanilla essence
250ml/8fl oz/1 cup maple syrup
whipped cream, to serve

1 Sift the flour and salt into a large bowl. Rub in the butter or white cooking fat until the mixture resembles breadcrumbs. Sprinkle with about 175ml/6fl oz/³/₄ cup water and mix until the dough holds together, adding a little more water if necessary. Gather into a ball. Place the dough in a sealed polythene bag and chill for at least 20 minutes. Preheat the oven to 220°C/425°F/Gas 7.

2 Peel the apples, then remove the cores, cutting from the stem end, without cutting through the base.

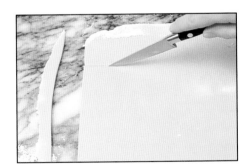

3 Roll out the pastry thinly. Cut squares almost large enough to enclose the apples, then brush the squares with egg white. Set an apple in the centre of each pastry square.

4 Combine the sugar, cream and vanilla essence in a small bowl. Spoon into the hollow of each apple.

5 Pull the points of the pastry squares up around the apples and moisten the edges where they overlap. Mould the pastry around the apples, pleating the top neatly. Do not cover the centre hollows of the apples. Crimp the edges to seal, if you prefer.

6 Set the apples in a large greased baking dish, at least 2cm/³/₄in apart. Bake for 30 minutes, then lower the oven temperature to 180°C/350°F/Gas 4 and continue baking for another 20 minutes more, until the pastry is golden brown and the apples are tender.

7 Transfer the dumplings to a serving dish. Mix the maple syrup with the juices in the baking dish and drizzle over the dumplings.

8 Serve the dumplings hot with whipped cream.

Cider Pie

Serves 6
175g/6oz/1½ cups plain flour
1.25ml/¼ tsp salt
10ml/2 tsp sugar
115g/4oz/½ cup cold butter or
   margarine
50ml/2fl oz/¼ cup or more iced water

For the filling
15g/½oz/1 tbsp butter
250ml/8fl oz/1 cup maple syrup
50ml/2fl oz/¼ cup water
600ml/1 pint/2½ cups cider
2 eggs, at room temperature,
   separated
5ml/1 tsp grated nutmeg

3 Meanwhile, place the cider in a saucepan and boil until only 175ml/6fl oz/¾ cup remains, then cool.

4 Roll out the pastry between two sheets of greaseproof or non-stick baking paper to 3mm/⅛in thickness. Use to line a 23cm/9in pie dish.

5 Trim around the edge, leaving a 1cm/½in overhang. Fold the overhang under to form the edge. Using a fork, press the edge to the rim of the dish and press up from under with your fingers at intervals to make a ruffle effect. Chill the pastry case for at least 20 minutes. Preheat the oven to 180°C/350°F/Gas 4.

6 To make the filling, place the butter, maple syrup, water and cider in a pan and simmer gently for 5–6 minutes. Remove the pan from the heat and leave the mixture to cool slightly, then whisk in the beaten egg yolks.

7 Whisk the egg whites in a large bowl, until they form stiff peaks. Add the cider mixture and fold gently together until evenly blended.

8 Pour the mixture into the prepared pastry case. Dust with the grated nutmeg. Bake the pie for 30–35 minutes, until the pastry is golden brown and the filling is well set and golden. Serve warm.

1 To make the pastry, sift the flour, salt and sugar into a bowl. Using a pastry blender or two knives, cut the butter or margarine into the dry ingredients as quickly as possible until the mixture resembles breadcrumbs.

2 Sprinkle the iced water over the flour mixture. Combine with a fork until the dough holds together. If the dough is too crumbly, add a little more water, 15ml/1 tbsp at a time. Gather the dough into a ball and flatten into a round. Place in a sealed polythene bag and chill for at least 20 minutes.

BLACKBERRY COBBLER

INGREDIENTS

Serves 8

750g/1¾lb blackberries
200g/7oz/1 cup caster sugar, plus 25g/
    1oz/2 tbsp caster sugar mixed with
    1.25ml/¼ tsp grated nutmeg
25g/1oz/3 tbsp plain flour
grated rind of 1 lemon

For the topping

225g/8oz/2 cups plain flour
200g/7oz/1 cup caster sugar
15ml/1 tbsp baking powder
pinch of salt
250ml/8fl oz/1 cup milk
115g/4oz/½ cup butter, melted

1 Preheat the oven to 180°C/350°F/
Gas 4. Place the blackberries, caster
sugar, flour and lemon rind in a large
mixing bowl. Stir gently to coat the
blackberries, then transfer to a 1.75
litre/3 pint/7½ cup baking dish.

2 To make the topping, sift the flour,
sugar, baking powder and salt into
a large bowl and set aside. Blend the
milk and butter in a large jug.

3 Gradually pour the milk mixture
into the dry ingredients and stir
until the mixture is just smooth.

4 Spoon the mixture over the
blackberries, spreading evenly.

5 Sprinkle the surface with the sugar
and nutmeg mixture. Bake for
about 50 minutes, until the topping is
set and lightly browned. Serve hot.

RHUBARB AND STRAWBERRY CRUMBLE

INGREDIENTS

Serves 4

225g/8oz strawberries, hulled and cut
    in half if large
450g/1lb rhubarb, cut into pieces
90g/3½oz/½ cup caster sugar
15ml/1 tbsp cornflour
85ml/3fl oz/⅓ cup fresh orange juice
115g/4oz/1 cup plain flour
75g/3oz/1 cup rolled oats
90g/3½oz/½ cup soft light brown
    sugar
2.5ml/½ tsp ground cinnamon
40g/1½oz/½ cup ground almonds
150g/5oz/10 tbsp cold butter
1 egg, lightly beaten

1 Preheat the oven to 180°C/350°F/
Gas 4, then mix together the
strawberries, rhubarb and sugar in a
1.75 litre/3 pint/7½ cup baking dish.

2 Blend the cornflour with the orange
juice in a small bowl, then pour this
mixture over the fruit and stir gently to
coat. Set the baking dish aside while
making the topping.

3 Toss together the flour, oats,
brown sugar, cinnamon and
almonds in a large bowl. Rub in the
butter using your fingertips until the
mixture resembles coarse breadcrumbs,
then stir in the beaten egg.

4 Spoon the oat mixture evenly over
the fruit and press down gently.
Bake for 50–60 minutes, until
browned. Serve the crumble warm.

Peanut Butter Tart

Serves 8
175g/6oz digestive biscuits, crushed
*50g/2oz/¼ cup soft light brown
    sugar*
*75g/3oz/6 tbsp butter or
    margarine, melted*
whipped cream or ice cream, to serve

For the filling
3 egg yolks
90g/3½oz/½ cup caster sugar
*50g/2oz/¼ cup soft light brown
    sugar*
25g/1oz/¼ cup cornflour
*600ml/1 pint/2½ cups canned
    evaporated milk*
*25g/1oz/2 tbsp unsalted butter or
    margarine*
7.5ml/1½ tsp vanilla essence
115g/4oz crunchy peanut butter
75g/3oz/¾ cup icing sugar

1 Preheat the oven to 180°C/350°F/
Gas 4. Grease a 23cm/9in pie dish.

2 Mix together the biscuit crumbs,
sugar and butter or margarine in a
bowl and blend well. Spread the
mixture in the prepared dish, pressing
the mixture evenly over the base and
sides with your fingertips.

3 Bake the crumb crust for 10
minutes. Remove from the oven
and leave to cool. Leave the oven on.

4 To make the filling, mix together
the egg yolks, caster and brown
sugars and cornflour in a heavy-based
saucepan using a wooden spoon.

5 Slowly whisk in the milk, then cook
over a medium heat for about 8–10
minutes, stirring constantly, until the
mixture thickens. Reduce the heat to
very low and cook for a further 3–4
minutes, until the mixture is very thick.

6 Beat in the butter or margarine and
the vanilla essence. Remove the pan
from the heat, then cover the surface
loosely with clear film and cool.

> **Cook's Tip**
> If preferred, use an equal amount
> of finely crushed ginger snaps in
> place of digestive biscuits for the
> crumb crust. Or make the pie
> with a ready-made pastry case.

7 Combine the peanut butter with
the icing sugar in a small bowl,
working with your fingertips to blend
the ingredients to the consistency of fine
breadcrumbs.

8 Sprinkle all but 45ml/3 tbsp of the
peanut butter crumbs evenly over
the base of the crumb crust.

9 Pour in the filling, spreading it into
an even layer, then sprinkle with
the remaining crumbs and bake for 15
minutes. Leave the pie to cool for at
least 1 hour. Serve with whipped cream
or ice cream.

BROWN SUGAR PIE

INGREDIENTS

Serves 8

175g/6oz/1½ cups plain flour
pinch of salt
20g/¾oz/2 tsp caster sugar
90ml/6 tbsp cold butter
50ml/2fl oz/¼ cup or more iced water

For the filling

25g/1oz/¼ cup plain flour, sifted
215g/7½oz/1 cup soft light brown
    sugar
2.5ml/½ tsp vanilla essence
350ml/12fl oz/1½ cups single cream
40g/1½oz/3 tbsp butter, cut into
    tiny pieces
large pinch of grated nutmeg

1 Sift the flour, salt and sugar into a bowl. Rub in the butter until the mixture resembles coarse breadcrumbs.

2 Sprinkle with the water and mix until the dough holds together. If it is too crumbly, slowly add more water, 15ml/1 tbsp at a time. Gather into a ball and flatten. Place in a sealed polythene bag and chill for at least 20 minutes.

3 Roll out the pastry to a 3mm/⅛in thickness and line a 23cm/9in pie dish or tin. Trim all around, leaving a 1cm/½in overhang. Fold it under and flute the edge. Chill for 30 minutes.

4 Preheat the oven to 220°C/425°F/ Gas 7. Line the pastry case with a piece of greaseproof paper that is 5cm/ 2in larger all around than the diameter of the dish or tin. Fill with dried beans and bake for 8–10 minutes, until the pastry has just set. Remove from the oven and carefully lift out the paper and the beans. Prick the base of the pastry case with a fork. Return to the oven and bake for 5 minutes more. Leave the pastry case to cool slightly before filling. Turn the oven down to 190°C/375°F/Gas 5.

5 To make the filling, mix together the flour and sugar in a small bowl using a fork. Spread this mixture in an even layer in the base of the pastry case.

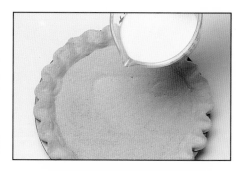

6 Stir the vanilla essence into the cream. Pour the flavoured cream over the flour and sugar mixture and gently swirl with a fork. Dot with the butter and sprinkle the nutmeg on top.

7 Cover the edge of the pie with foil strips to prevent overbrowning. Place on a baking sheet and bake for about 45 minutes, until the filling is golden brown and set to the touch. Serve the pie at room temperature.

BAKED PEACHES WITH RASPBERRY SAUCE

INGREDIENTS

Serves 6

40g/1¹/₂oz/3 tbsp unsalted butter, at
room temperature
40g/1¹/₂oz/¹/₄ cup caster sugar
1 egg, beaten
40g/1¹/₂oz/¹/₂ cup ground almonds
6 ripe peaches

For the sauce

150g/5oz/1 cup raspberries
15g/¹/₂oz/1 tbsp icing sugar
15ml/1 tbsp raspberry liqueur
raspberries and bay leaves,
to decorate

3 Place the peach halves on a baking sheet (if necessary, secure with crumpled foil to keep them steady) and fill the hollow in each peach half with the almond mixture.

4 Bake for about 30 minutes, until the almond filling is puffed and golden and the peaches are very tender.

5 Meanwhile, to make the sauce, place the raspberries, icing sugar and liqueur in a food processor or blender. Add the reserved peach flesh and process until smooth. Press through a sieve to remove the seeds.

6 Leave the peaches to cool slightly, then serve with the raspberry sauce. Decorate each serving with a few raspberries and bay leaves.

1 Beat the butter with the sugar until light and fluffy, then beat in the egg. Add the ground almonds and beat just enough to blend together well.

2 Preheat the oven to 180°C/350°F/ Gas 4. Halve the peaches and remove the stones. With a spoon, scrape out a little of the flesh from each peach half, slightly enlarging the hollow left by the stone. Reserve the excess peach flesh for the sauce.

Peach and Blueberry Pie

INGREDIENTS

Serves 8

225g/8oz/2 cups plain flour
pinch of salt
10ml/2 tsp sugar
150g/5oz/10 tbsp cold butter or
* margarine*
1 egg yolk
50ml/2fl oz/¼ cup or more iced water
30ml/2 tbsp milk, to glaze

For the filling

450g/1lb fresh peaches, peeled, stoned
* and sliced*
275g/10oz/2 cups fresh blueberries
150g/5oz/¾ cup caster sugar
30ml/2 tbsp fresh lemon juice
40g/1½oz/⅓ cup plain flour
large pinch of grated nutmeg
25g/1oz/2 tbsp butter or margarine, cut
* into tiny pieces*

1 To make the pastry, sift the flour, salt and sugar into a bowl. Rub the butter or margarine into the dry ingredients as quickly as possible until the mixture resembles coarse breadcrumbs.

2 Mix the egg yolk with the iced water and sprinkle over the flour mixture. Combine with a fork until the dough holds together. If the dough is too crumbly, add a little more water, 15ml/1 tbsp at a time. Gather the dough into a ball and flatten into a round. Place in a sealed polythene bag and chill for at least 20 minutes.

3 Roll out two-thirds of the pastry between two sheets of greaseproof paper to a thickness of about 3mm/ ⅛in. Use to line a 23cm/9in pie dish. Trim all around, leaving a 1cm/½in overhang. Fold the overhang under to form the edge. Using a fork, press the edge to the rim of the pie tin.

4 Gather the trimmings and remaining pastry into a ball, and roll out to a thickness of about 5mm/ ¼in. Using a pastry wheel or sharp knife, cut into long, 1cm/½in wide strips. Chill both the pastry case and the strips of pastry for at least 20 minutes. Meanwhile, preheat the oven to 200°C/ 400°F/Gas 6.

5 Line the pastry case with greaseproof paper and fill with dried beans. Bake for 7–10 minutes, until the pastry is just set. Remove from the oven and carefully lift out the paper with the beans. Prick the base of the pastry case with a fork, then return to the oven and bake for a further 5 minutes. Allow to cool slightly before filling. Leave the oven on.

6 Place the peach slices and blueberries in a bowl and stir in the sugar, lemon juice, flour and nutmeg. Spoon the fruit mixture into the pastry case. Dot the top with the pieces of butter or margarine.

7 Weave a lattice top with the chilled pastry strips, pressing the ends to the edge of the baked pastry case. Brush the strips with the milk.

8 Bake the pie for 15 minutes. Reduce the oven temperature to 180°C/350°F/Gas 4, and continue baking for another 30 minutes, until the filling is tender and bubbling and the pastry lattice is golden. If the pastry becomes too brown, cover loosely with a piece of foil. Serve the pie warm or at room temperature.

Apple Brown Betty

Serves 6

50g/2oz/1 cup fresh white breadcrumbs
175g/6oz/³⁄₄ cup soft light brown sugar
2.5ml/¹⁄₂ tsp ground cinnamon
1.25ml/¹⁄₄ tsp ground cloves
1.25ml/¹⁄₄ tsp grated nutmeg
50g/2oz/4 tbsp butter
1kg/2lb cooking apples
juice of 1 lemon
25g/1oz/¹⁄₃ cup finely chopped walnuts
cream or ice cream, to serve

3 Peel, core, and slice the apples. Toss immediately with the lemon juice to prevent the apple slices from turning brown.

4 Sprinkle 30–45ml/2–3 tbsp of breadcrumbs into the prepared dish. Cover with one-third of the apples and sprinkle with one-third of the sugar and spice mixture. Add another layer of breadcrumbs and dot with one-third of the butter. Repeat the layers two more times, ending with a layer of breadcrumbs. Sprinkle with the nuts, and dot with the remaining butter.

5 Bake for 35–40 minutes, until the apples are tender and the top is golden brown. Serve warm with cream or ice cream, if you like.

1 Preheat the grill. Spread out the breadcrumbs on a baking sheet and toast under the grill until golden, stirring frequently to colour them evenly. Set aside. Preheat the oven to 190°C/375°F/Gas 5. Butter a large deep ovenproof dish.

2 Mix the sugar with the cinnamon, cloves and nutmeg. Cut the butter into tiny pieces, then set aside.

BAKED APPLES WITH APRICOTS

INGREDIENTS

Serves 6

*75g/3oz/¹⁄₂ cup chopped, ready-to-eat
  dried apricots*
50g/2oz/¹⁄₂ cup chopped walnuts
5ml/1 tsp grated lemon rind
1.25ml/¹⁄₄ tsp ground cinnamon
*90g/3¹⁄₂oz/¹⁄₂ cup soft light brown
  sugar*
*25g/1oz/2 tbsp butter, at room
  temperature*
6 large eating apples
15ml/1 tbsp melted butter

1 Place the apricots, walnuts, lemon rind and cinnamon in a bowl. Add the sugar and butter and stir until thoroughly mixed.

2 Preheat the oven to 190°C/375°F/ Gas 5. Core the apples, without cutting all the way through to the base. Peel the top of each apple and slightly widen the top of each opening to make room for the filling.

3 Spoon the filling into the apples, packing it down lightly.

4 Place the stuffed apples in an ovenproof dish large enough to hold them comfortably side by side.

5 Brush the apples with the melted butter. Bake for 40–45 minutes, until they are tender. Serve hot.

RHUBARB PIE

INGREDIENTS

Serves 6
175g/6oz/1½ cups plain flour
2.5ml/½ tsp salt
10ml/2 tsp caster sugar
75g/3oz/6 tbsp cold butter or margarine
50ml/2fl oz/¼ cup or more iced water
30ml/2 tbsp single cream

For the filling
1kg/2lb fresh rhubarb, cut into 2.5cm/
   1in slices
30ml/2 tbsp cornflour
1 egg
275g/10oz/1½ cups caster sugar
15ml/1 tbsp grated orange rind

1 To make the pastry, sift the flour, salt and sugar into a bowl. Using a pastry blender or two knives, cut the butter or margarine into the dry ingredients as quickly as possible until the mixture resembles breadcrumbs.

2 Sprinkle with the iced water and mix until the dough holds together. If the dough is too crumbly, add a little more water, 15ml/1 tbsp at a time.

COOK'S TIP
Use milk in place of the whipping cream to glaze the pie, or for a crisp crust, brush with water and sprinkle with caster sugar instead.

3 Gather the dough into a ball, flatten into a round, place in a polythene bag and chill for 20 minutes.

4 Roll out the pastry between two sheets of greaseproof paper to a 3mm/⅛in thickness. Use to line a 23cm/9in pie dish or tin. Trim all around, leaving a 1cm/½in overhang. Fold the overhang under the edge and flute. Chill the pastry case and trimmings for at least 30 minutes.

5 To make the filling, put the rhubarb in a bowl, sprinkle with the cornflour and toss to coat.

6 Preheat the oven to 220°C/425°F/Gas 7. Beat the egg with the sugar in a bowl, then mix in the orange rind.

7 Stir the sugar mixture into the rhubarb and mix well, then spoon the fruit into the pastry case.

8 Roll out the pastry trimmings. Stamp out decorative shapes with a biscuit cutter or cut shapes with a small knife, using a cardboard template as a guide, if you prefer.

9 Arrange the pastry shapes on top of the pie. Brush the shapes and the edge of the pastry case with cream.

10 Bake the pie for 30 minutes. Reduce the oven temperature to 160°C/325°F/Gas 3 and continue baking for a further 15–20 minutes, until the pastry is golden brown and the rhubarb is tender. Serve hot with cream.

COLD DESSERTS

There's a delectable selection of recipes in this section: stunning creations for dinner parties, and quick and easy desserts for family meals. For special occasions, recipes that can be prepared ahead are a real boon, so opt for the classic Pears in Red Wine, or, if you have plenty of time for preparation, try the White Chocolate Parfait, a distinctly different frozen dessert. Cheesecakes are popular at any event and the creamy American-style Blueberry Cheesecake here is quite delicious. In the summer, fruit salads make the perfect finish to a meal and there are two colourful and refreshing recipes to choose from – for a change, bake a tangy Lemon Ring Cake or Pecan Pralines to accompany them. If you are cooking for children, treat them to a simply scrumptious Chocolate Fudge Sundae.

LIME SORBET

Serves 4
185g/6¹/₂oz/1¹/₄ cups granulated sugar
600ml/1 pint/2¹/₂ cups water
grated rind of 1 lime
175ml/6fl oz/³/₄ cup freshly squeezed
  lime juice
15–30ml/1–2 tbsp fresh lemon juice
icing sugar, to taste
shreds of lime rind, to decorate

1 Place the granulated sugar and water in a small pan. Cook without stirring, over a medium heat. When the sugar has dissolved, boil for 5–6 minutes, then remove the pan from the heat and leave to cool.

2 Mix together the cooled sugar syrup and lime rind and juice in a measuring jug or bowl. Stir well. Taste and adjust the flavour by adding lemon juice or icing sugar, if necessary. Take care not to over-sweeten.

3 Freeze the lime mixture in an ice cream maker, following the manufacturer's instructions.

4 If you do not have an ice cream maker, pour the mixture into a metal or plastic freezer container and freeze for about 3 hours, until slushy.

5 Remove the sorbet from the container and chop roughly. Place in a food processor and process until smooth. Return the mixture to the freezer container and freeze again until firm. Process the sorbet once more, then freeze until firm. Scoop into balls and serve in pretty dessert dishes decorated with shreds of lime rind.

COOK'S TIP
If using an ice cream maker for this sorbet, check the manufacturer's instructions to find out the freezing capacity. If necessary, halve the recipe.

POACHED PEARS IN RED WINE

INGREDIENTS

Serves 4

1 bottle red wine
150g/5oz/¾ cup caster sugar
45ml/3 tbsp honey
juice of ½ lemon
1 cinnamon stick
1 vanilla pod, split open lengthways
5cm/2in piece orange rind
1 clove
1 black peppercorn
4 firm, ripe pears
whipped cream or soured cream,
   to serve

1 Place the wine, sugar, honey, lemon juice, cinnamon stick, vanilla pod, orange rind, clove and peppercorn in a saucepan just large enough to hold the pears standing upright. Heat gently, stirring occasionally, until the sugar has completely dissolved.

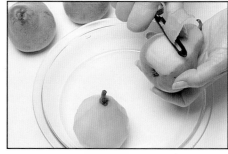

2 Meanwhile, peel the pears, leaving the stem intact. Take a thin slice off the base of each pear so that it will stand square and upright.

3 Place the pears in the wine mixture, then simmer, uncovered for 20–35 minutes depending on size and ripeness, until the pears are just tender; be careful not to overcook.

4 Carefully transfer the pears to a bowl using a slotted spoon. Continue to boil the poaching liquid until reduced by about half. Leave to cool, then strain the cooled liquid over the pears and chill for at least 3 hours.

5 Place the pears in four individual serving dishes and spoon over a little of the red wine syrup. Serve with whipped cream or soured cream.

CHOCOLATE FUDGE SUNDAES

INGREDIENTS

Serves 4

4 scoops each vanilla and coffee
  ice cream
2 small ripe bananas, sliced
whipped cream
toasted flaked almonds

For the sauce

50g/2oz/¼ cup soft light brown
  sugar
120ml/4fl oz/½ cup golden syrup
45ml/3 tbsp strong black coffee
5ml/1 tsp ground cinnamon
150g/5oz plain chocolate, chopped
85ml/3fl oz/⅓ cup whipping cream
45ml/3 tbsp coffee liqueur (optional)

1 To make the sauce, place the sugar, syrup, coffee and cinnamon in a heavy-based saucepan. Bring to the boil, then boil for about 5 minutes, stirring constantly.

2 Turn off the heat and stir in the chocolate. When melted and smooth, stir in the cream and liqueur, if using. Leave the sauce to cool slightly. If made ahead, reheat the sauce gently until just warm.

3 Fill four glasses with a scoop each of vanilla and coffee ice cream.

4 Scatter the sliced bananas over the ice cream. Pour the warm fudge sauce over the bananas, then top each sundae with a generous swirl of whipped cream. Sprinkle with toasted almonds and serve at once.

COFFEE, VANILLA AND CHOCOLATE STRIPE

─── INGREDIENTS ───

Serves 6
285g/10½oz/1½ cups caster sugar
90ml/6 tbsp cornflour
900ml/1½ pints/4 cups milk
3 egg yolks
75g/3oz/6 tbsp unsalted butter, at
  room temperature
20ml/generous 1 tbsp instant
  coffee powder
10ml/2 tsp vanilla essence
30ml/2 tbsp cocoa powder
whipped cream, to serve

1 To make the coffee layer, place 90g/3½oz/½ cup of the sugar and 30ml/2 tbsp of the cornflour in a heavy-based saucepan. Gradually add one third of the milk, whisking until well blended. Over a medium heat, whisk in one of the egg yolks and bring to the boil, whisking. Boil for 1 minute.

2 Remove the pan from the heat. Stir in 25g/1oz/2 tbsp of the butter and the instant coffee powder. Set aside in the pan to cool slightly.

3 Divide the coffee mixture among six wine glasses. Smooth the tops before the mixture sets.

4 Wipe any dribbles on the insides and outsides of the glasses with damp kitchen paper.

5 To make the vanilla layer, place half of the remaining sugar and cornflour in a heavy-based saucepan. Whisk in 300ml/½ pint/1⅓ cups of the milk. Over a medium heat, whisk in another egg yolk and bring to the boil, whisking. Boil for 1 minute.

6 Remove the pan from the heat and stir in 25g/1oz/2 tbsp of the butter and the vanilla. Leave to cool slightly, then spoon into the glasses on top of the coffee layer. Smooth the tops and wipe the glasses with kitchen paper.

7 To make the chocolate layer, place the remaining sugar and cornflour in a heavy-based saucepan. Gradually whisk in the remaining milk and continue whisking until blended. Over a medium heat, whisk in the last egg yolk and bring to the boil, whisking constantly. Boil for 1 minute. Remove from the heat, stir in the remaining butter and the cocoa. Leave to cool slightly, then spoon into the glasses on top of the vanilla layer. Chill until set.

8 Pipe swirls of whipped cream on top of each dessert before serving.

COOK'S TIP
For a special occasion, prepare the vanilla layer using a fresh vanilla pod. Choose a plump, supple pod and split it down the centre with a sharp knife. Add to the mixture with the milk and discard the pod before spooning the mixture into the glasses. The flavour will be more pronounced and the pudding will have pretty brown speckles from the vanilla seeds.

White Chocolate Parfait

Serves 10
225g/8oz white chocolate, chopped
600ml/1 pint/2½ cups whipping cream
120ml/4fl oz/½ cup milk
10 egg yolks
15ml/1 tbsp caster sugar
25g/1oz/½ cup desiccated coconut
*120ml/4fl oz/½ cup canned sweetened
  coconut milk*
150g/5oz unsalted macadamia nuts

For the chocolate icing
225g/8oz plain chocolate
75g/3oz/6 tbsp butter
20ml/1 generous tbsp golden syrup
175ml/6fl oz/¾ cup whipping cream
curls of fresh coconut, to decorate

1 Line the base and sides of a 1.4 litre/2⅓ pint/6 cup terrine mould (25 × 10cm/10 × 4in) with clear film.

2 Place the white chocolate and 50ml/2fl oz/¼ cup of the cream in the top of a double boiler or in a heatproof bowl set over hot water. Stir until melted and smooth. Set aside.

3 Put 250ml/8fl oz/1 cup of the cream and the milk in a pan and bring to boiling point.

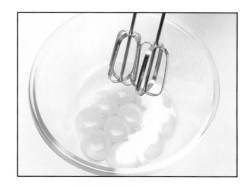

4 Meanwhile, whisk the egg yolks and caster sugar together in a large bowl, until thick and pale.

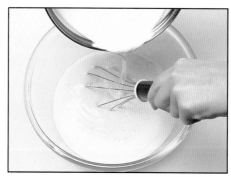

5 Add the hot cream mixture to the yolks, beating constantly. Pour back into the saucepan and cook over a low heat for 2–3 minutes, until thickened. Stir constantly and do not boil. Remove the pan from the heat.

6 Add the melted chocolate, desiccated coconut and coconut milk, then stir well and leave to cool.

7 Whip the remaining cream until thick, then fold into the chocolate and coconut mixture.

8 Put 475ml/16fl oz/2 cups of the parfait mixture in the prepared mould and spread evenly. Cover and freeze for about 2 hours, until just firm. Cover the remaining mixture and chill.

9 Scatter the macadamia nuts evenly over the frozen parfait. Pour in the remaining parfait mixture. Cover the terrine and freeze for 6–8 hours or overnight, until the parfait is firm.

10 To make the icing, melt the chocolate with the butter and syrup in the top of a double boiler set over hot water. Stir occasionally.

11 Heat the cream in a saucepan, until just simmering, then stir into the chocolate mixture. Remove the pan from the heat and leave to cool until lukewarm.

12 To turn out the parfait, wrap the terrine in a hot towel and set it upside down on a plate. Lift off the terrine mould, then peel off the clear film. Place the parfait on a rack over a baking sheet and pour the chocolate icing evenly over the top. Working quickly, smooth the icing down the sides with a palette knife. Leave to set slightly, then freeze for a further 3–4 hours. Cut into slices using a knife dipped in hot water. Serve, decorated with coconut curls.

Coconut Fruit Salad

INGREDIENTS

Serves 6
4 large oranges
1 fresh ripe pineapple
1 coconut
icing sugar (optional)
strips of fresh coconut, to decorate

1 Using a small sharp knife, cut the peel and pith from the oranges, working over a bowl to catch the juice. Slice each orange horizontally into very thin rounds and place them in the bowl with the orange juice.

2 Cut away all the peel from the pineapple and cut into quarters lengthways. Remove and discard the core, then cut into thin slices.

3 Carefully pierce the "eyes" of the coconut with a screwdriver or other pointed implement. Drain off the liquid. Using a heavy hammer, crack the shell until it can be opened. Prise out the white flesh with a blunt knife. Peel the dark brown skin from the coconut flesh and shred the flesh using the coarse blade of a grater or food processor.

4 To assemble the dessert, layer the fruits and coconut alternately in a glass serving bowl. Sprinkle the layers occasionally with a little icing sugar, if you prefer a sweeter dessert. Serve immediately or chill before eating. Decorate with strips of fresh coconut before serving.

Pecan Pralines

INGREDIENTS

Makes about 30
300g/11oz/1½ cups soft light brown sugar
300g/11oz/1½ cups soft dark brown sugar
1.25ml/¼ tsp salt
120ml/4fl oz/½ cup milk
120ml/4fl oz/½ cup single cream
25g/1oz/2 tbsp butter or margarine
5ml/1 tsp vanilla essence
115g/4oz/1 cup pecan nut pieces or halves

COOK'S TIP
To test for the soft ball stage without a sugar thermometer, drop a small amount of the syrup into iced water. It should form a ball that will hold its shape and flatten readily when picked up between the fingers.

1 Mix together the sugars, salt, milk and cream in a heavy saucepan. Place over a medium heat and bring to the boil, stirring constantly. Cover the pan and cook, without stirring, for about 3 minutes, until crystals no longer form on the sides of the pan.

2 Uncover the pan and cook over a medium heat, without stirring, to the soft ball stage, 119°C/238°F on a sugar thermometer.

3 Remove the pan from the heat and beat in the butter or margarine with a wooden spoon. Continue beating until the mixture is smooth and creamy and the temperature of the mixture comes down to 43°C/110°F. Beat in the vanilla essence and the nuts.

4 Using two spoons, drop the mixture by the spoonful on to a baking sheet lined with non-stick baking paper. When cool, store in an airtight container with greaseproof paper between each of the layers.

CARAMEL CUSTARD

INGREDIENTS

Serves 8–10
800ml/1⅓ pints/3½ cups milk
120ml/4fl oz/½ cup single cream
200g/7oz/1 cup caster sugar
1 cinnamon stick
8 size 1 eggs
5ml/1 tsp vanilla essence

For the caramel
130g/4½oz/⅔ cup granulated sugar
50ml/2fl oz/¼ cup water

1 Place the milk, cream, sugar and cinnamon in a pan. Bring just to the boil, stirring. Remove from the heat, cover and set aside for 30 minutes.

2 Make the caramel; place the sugar and water in a small, heavy-based saucepan set over a medium-high heat.

3 Bring to the boil, then simmer until the syrup begins to colour; do not stir. When the syrup is a deep golden brown, dip the base of the pan in cold water to stop it cooking.

4 Quickly pour the caramel syrup into a 2.25 litre/4 pint soufflé dish and tilt to coat the base evenly.

5 Preheat the oven to 180°C/350°F/ Gas 4. Reheat the milk mixture until just warm and remove the cinnamon stick. Place the eggs and vanilla essence in a large bowl and mix together. Pour the milk mixture over the egg mixture, stirring constantly.

6 Place the caramel-coated soufflé dish in a large baking dish and add enough hot water to come 5cm/2in up the side of the soufflé dish. Pour the egg mixture through a sieve into the soufflé dish. Cover with foil.

7 Bake for 40–45 minutes until the custard is just set. Cool in the water bath, then chill for at least 4 hours.

8 To serve, run a knife around the inside of the soufflé dish. Place a plate on top and turn over to release the custard. Spoon any remaining caramel on to the custard.

CINNAMON AND COCONUT RICE

Serves 4–6
40g/1½oz/¼ cup raisins
475ml/16fl oz/2 cups water
225g/8oz/1 cup short grain rice
1 cinnamon stick
25g/1oz/2 tbsp caster sugar
475ml/16fl oz/2 cups milk
250ml/8fl oz/1 cup canned sweetened
   coconut milk
2.5ml/½ tsp vanilla essence
15ml/1 tbsp butter
25g/1oz/⅓ cup desiccated coconut
ground cinnamon for sprinkling

1 Soak the raisins in a small bowl in enough water to cover.

2 Bring the water to the boil in a medium-sized saucepan. Stir in the rice, cinnamon stick and sugar. Return to the boil, then lower the heat, cover, and simmer gently for 15–20 minutes, until the liquid is absorbed.

3 Meanwhile, blend the milk, coconut milk and vanilla essence together in a bowl. Drain the raisins.

4 Remove the cinnamon stick from the pan of rice. Add the raisins and the milk and coconut mixture and stir to mix. Continue cooking, covered and stirring often, for about 20 minutes, until the mixture is just thick. Do not overcook the rice.

5 Preheat the grill. Transfer the rice to a flameproof serving dish. Dot with the butter and sprinkle with coconut. Grill about 13cm/5in from the heat for about 3–5 minutes, until the top is just browned. Sprinkle with cinnamon. Serve warm, or cold with cream, if you like.

BLUEBERRY CHEESECAKE

1 To make the crumb case, put the hazelnuts in a large bowl. Sift in the flour and salt and stir to mix. Set aside.

COOK'S TIP
The cheesecake can be prepared one day in advance, but add the fruit shortly before serving. For a change, pipe swirls of cream around the edge before adding the fruit, if you like.

2 Beat the butter with the brown sugar until light and fluffy, then beat in the egg yolk. Gradually fold in the nut mixture, in three batches.

3 Using the back of a spoon, press the mixture into a deep, greased 23cm/9in pie dish or tin, spreading it evenly over the base and sides. Form a rim around the top edge that is slightly thicker than the sides. Cover and chill for at least 30 minutes. Preheat the oven to 180°C/350°F/Gas 4.

4 To make the topping, mix the blueberries, honey, 15ml/1 tbsp of the caster sugar and 5ml/1 tsp of the lemon juice in a heavy-based saucepan. Cook over a low heat for 5–7 minutes, stirring occasionally, until the berries have given off some liquid but still retain their shape. Remove the pan from the heat and set aside.

5 Bake the crumb case in the oven for 15 minutes, then remove and leave to cool while making the filling.

6 Beat together the cream cheese and remaining caster sugar in a bowl until light and fluffy. Beat in the egg and the remaining lemon juice, then add the cream and beat until thoroughly blended.

7 Pour the cheese mixture into the crumb case and spread evenly. Bake for 20–25 minutes, until just set.

8 Leave the cheesecake to cool completely on a wire rack, then cover and chill for at least 1 hour.

9 Spread the blueberry mixture evenly over the top of the cheesecake. Serve slightly chilled or at room temperature.

LEMON RING CAKE

INGREDIENTS

Serves 8–10
275g/10oz/1¼ cups unsalted butter,
    at room temperature
350g/12oz/1¾ cups caster sugar
6 eggs
grated rind and juice of 1 large lemon
300g/11oz/2⅓ cups plain flour,
    sifted with a pinch of salt
icing sugar, for dusting

1 Preheat the oven to 180°C/350°F/
Gas 4. Grease a 23cm/9in ring
mould. Beat the butter until it is soft
and creamy. Gradually add the sugar
and continue beating until fluffy.

2 Beat in the eggs, one at a time,
beating well after each addition.
Beat in the lemon rind and juice, then
fold in the flour and salt gradually.

3 Pour the batter into the prepared
mould and smooth the surface.

4 Bake for 40–50 minutes, until a
skewer inserted in the centre comes
out clean. Leave to cool for 10 minutes
before turning out on to a wire rack.

5 When the cake is completely cold,
dust it with sifted icing sugar.

PIÑA COLADA FRUIT SALAD

INGREDIENTS

Serves 4
1 large pineapple
2 kiwi fruit
50g/2oz/¼ cup slivered fresh coconut
30ml/2 tbsp fresh lime juice
5ml/1 tsp caster sugar
15–30ml/1–2 tbsp rum
8 large strawberries, halved

1 Cut a thick slice from one long side
of the pineapple, not cutting into
the crown of leaves.

2 Using a sharp spoon or a grapefruit
knife, scoop out the flesh from the
pineapple, taking care not to puncture
the skin. Cut away and discard the core.
Set the pineapple boat aside.

3 Chop the scooped-out pineapple
flesh into bite-size pieces, reserving
any juice, and place in a bowl.

4 Peel the kiwi fruits and cut into
thick slices. Add the kiwi fruit and
coconut to the pineapple pieces.

5 Place the lime juice, sugar and rum,
to taste, in a small jug or bowl. Stir
to blend, then pour over the fruit. Toss
well to coat all the fruit, then cover and
chill for about 1 hour.

6 When ready to serve, spoon the
fruit mixture into the pineapple
boat. Decorate with the strawberry
halves and serve immediately.

BAKED MAPLE CUSTARD

INGREDIENTS

Serves 6
3 eggs
120ml/4fl oz/½ cup maple syrup
600ml/1 pint/2½ cups milk
large pinch of grated nutmeg

COOK'S TIP
Baking delicate mixtures such as custards in a water bath helps protect them from uneven heating which could make them rubbery.

1 Preheat the oven to 180°C/350°F/ Gas 4. Place the eggs, maple syrup, milk and nutmeg in a large bowl and whisk thoroughly.

2 Place six individual ramekins in a roasting tin half-filled with hot water. Pour the custard mixture into the ramekins. Bake for ¾–1 hour, until the custards are set. To test the custards are cooked, insert the blade of a knife in the centre: it should come out clean. Serve the custards chilled.

CRANBERRY ICE

INGREDIENTS

Makes about 1.4 litres/2⅓ pints/6 cups
1kg/2lb/8 cups fresh or frozen
  cranberries
475ml/16fl oz/2 cups water
350g/12oz/1¾ cups caster sugar
generous pinch grated orange rind
30ml/2 tbsp fresh orange juice

1 Check the manufacturer's instructions for your ice cream maker, if using one, to find out its capacity. If necessary, halve the recipe.

2 Carefully pick over and wash the cranberries. Discard those that are blemished or soft.

3 Place the cranberries in a stainless-steel saucepan with the water and bring to the boil. Reduce the heat and simmer for about 15 minutes, until the cranberries are tender.

4 Press the cranberry mixture through a fine-mesh nylon sieve set over a bowl. Return the purée to the pan, add the sugar and stir until the sugar is dissolved. Bring to the boil and simmer for 5 minutes. Stir in the orange rind and juice. Remove the pan from the heat and leave the cranberry mixture to cool to room temperature.

5 To freeze in an ice cream maker, pour the cranberry mixture into the machine and freeze following the manufacturer's instructions.

6 If you do not have an ice cream maker, pour the mixture into a metal or plastic freezer container and freeze for about 3 hours, until softly set. Remove the frozen cranberry mixture from the container and chop roughly. Place in a food processor and process until smooth. Return the mixture to the freezer container and freeze again until firm. Repeat this freezing and chopping process two or three times, then freeze once more until firm.

CAKES AND BAKES

Home-baked cakes are a delight to make and delicious to eat! There are recipes here for lovely large cakes to serve as a tea-time treat; rich sponges sandwiched with creamy, smooth fillings, a scrumptious moist Frosted Walnut Cake, and a gorgeous Banana and Lemon Cake. If you love chocolate, then there are real delights in store: you'll find a gorgeous chocolate-iced Custard Layer Cake, an irresistible Mississippi Mud Cake, and a moist and more-ish Chocolate Cake with Banana Sauce which you can serve as a pudding, if you like. Fruit and Nut Turnovers would also double as a dessert – they are a bit of a fiddle to make, but well worth the effort. If you are baking for a coffee morning, try the simple-to-prepare Chocolate Nut Bars, Spicy Aniseed Biscuits or Spicy Apple Cookies.

SWEET POTATO SCONES

Makes about 24

150g/5oz/1¼ cups plain flour
20ml/4 tsp baking powder
5ml/1 tsp salt
15g/½oz/1 tbsp soft light brown
* sugar*
150g/5oz/¾ cup mashed cooked
* sweet potatoes*
150ml/¼ pint/⅔ cup milk
50g/2oz/4 tbsp butter or margarine,
* melted*

1 Preheat oven to 230°C/450°F/Gas 8. Sift the flour, baking powder and salt into a bowl. Add the sugar and mix.

3 Add the sifted flour to the sweet potato mixture and stir together to make a dough. Turn on to a lightly floured surface and knead lightly for 1–2 minutes, until soft and pliable.

2 In a separate bowl, mix the mashed sweet potatoes with the milk and melted butter or margarine. Beat well until evenly blended.

4 Roll or pat out the dough to a 1cm/½in thickness. Cut out rounds using a 4cm/1½in biscuit cutter.

5 Arrange the rounds on a greased baking sheet. Bake for about 15 minutes until risen and lightly golden. Serve the scones warm.

CUSTARD LAYER CAKE

INGREDIENTS

Serves 8
225g/8oz/2 cups plain flour
15ml/1 tbsp baking powder
pinch of salt
115g/4oz/½ cup butter, at room
    temperature
200g/7oz/1 cup caster sugar
2 eggs
5ml/1 tsp vanilla essence
175ml/6fl oz/¾ cup milk

For the filling
250ml/8fl oz/1 cup milk
3 egg yolks
90g/3½oz/½ cup caster sugar
25g/1oz/¼ cup plain flour
15g/½oz/1 tbsp butter
15ml/1 tbsp brandy or 15ml/1 tsp
    vanilla essence

For the chocolate icing
25g/1oz plain chocolate
25g/1oz/2 tbsp butter or margarine
50g/2oz/½ cup icing sugar, plus extra
    for dusting
2.5ml/½ tsp vanilla essence
about 15ml/1 tbsp hot water

1 Preheat the oven to 190°C/375°F/
Gas 5. Grease two deep round cake
tins, and line the bases of each with
rounds of greased greaseproof paper.

2 Sift together the flour, baking
powder and salt. Beat the butter
and caster sugar together in a separate
bowl, until light and fluffy. Add the
eggs one at a time, beating well after
each addition. Stir in the vanilla
essence. Add the milk and dry
ingredients alternately, mixing only
enough to blend thoroughly. Do not
over-beat the mixture.

3 Divide the cake mixture between
the prepared tins and smooth the
top evenly. Bake for about 25 minutes,
until a skewer inserted in the centre
comes out clean.

4 Meanwhile, make the filling, heat
the milk in a small saucepan to
boiling point. Remove from the heat.

5 Whisk the egg yolks in a heatproof
mixing bowl. Gradually add the
sugar and continue whisking, until the
mixture is thick and pale yellow. Beat in
the sifted flour.

6 Pour the hot milk into the egg yolk
mixture in a steady stream, beating
constantly. Place the bowl over a pan of
boiling water, or pour the mixture into
the top of a double boiler. Heat, stirring
constantly, until thickened. Cook for a
further 2 minutes, then remove from the
heat. Stir in the butter and brandy or
vanilla essence. Set aside and leave until
cold, stirring frequently.

7 When the cakes have completely
cooled, place one on a serving plate
and carefully spread over the custard
filling in a thick layer using a large
palette knife. Place the other cake on
top. Smooth the edge of the custard
filling with a small palette knife or
teaspoon to remove excess custard and
give an attractive tidy finish to the cake.

8 To make the icing, melt the
chocolate with the butter or
margarine in the top of a double boiler
set over a pan of hot water. When
smooth, remove from the heat and beat
in the sugar to make a thick paste. Add
the vanilla essence, then beat in a little
of the hot water. If the icing does not
have a spreadable consistency, add
more water, 5ml/1 tsp at a time.

9 Using a large palette knife, spread
the icing evenly over the top of the
cake. Dust the top with icing sugar.
(Since it has a custard filling, store any
leftover cake in the fridge.)

Chocolate Cake with Banana Sauce

INGREDIENTS

Serves 6
115g/4oz plain chocolate, chopped
115g/4oz/1/2 cup unsalted butter
15ml/1 tbsp instant coffee powder
5 eggs, separated
200g/7oz/1 cup caster sugar
115g/4oz/1 cup plain flour
10ml/2 tsp ground cinnamon

For the sauce
4 ripe bananas
50g/2oz/1/4 cup soft dark brown
  sugar
15ml/1 tbsp fresh lemon juice
175ml/6fl oz/3/4 cup whipping
  cream
15ml/1 tbsp rum (optional)

1 Preheat the oven to 180°C/350°F/
Gas 4. Grease and base-line a
20cm/8in round cake tin.

2 Place the chocolate and butter in a
heatproof bowl set over a saucepan
of hot water and stir until melted.
Remove the bowl from the pan and stir
in the coffee powder. Set aside.

3 Whisk the egg yolks with the sugar
until thick and pale. Add the
chocolate and butter mixture and beat
on a low speed just until the mixtures
are blended evenly.

4 Sift together the flour and ground
cinnamon into a bowl.

5 Whisk the egg whites in a clean
bowl, until they hold stiff peaks.

6 Stir a spoonful of egg white into the
chocolate mixture to lighten it,
then fold in the remainder in three
batches, alternating with the flour.

7 Pour the mixture into the prepared
tin. Bake for 40–50 minutes, until a
skewer inserted in the centre comes out
clean. Turn out the cake on to a wire
rack. Preheat the grill.

8 To make the sauce, slice the
bananas into a shallow, heatproof
dish. Add the brown sugar and lemon
juice and stir to blend. Place under the
grill and cook for about 8 minutes,
stirring occasionally, until the sugar is
caramelized and bubbling.

9 Turn the bananas into a bowl and
mash with a fork until almost
smooth. Add the cream and rum, if
using. Serve the cake and sauce warm.

Variation
For a special occasion, top the cake
slices with a scoop of ice cream
(rum and raisin, chocolate or
vanilla) before adding the banana
sauce. The cake would then make
a delicious dessert for at least
eight people.

MISSISSIPPI MUD CAKE

INGREDIENTS

Serves 8–10

225g/8oz/2 cups plain flour
pinch of salt
5ml/1 tsp baking powder
300ml/½ pint/1¼ cups strong
    black coffee
45ml/3 tbsp brandy
150g/5oz bitter or plain chocolate,
    broken into squares
225g/8oz/1 cup butter or margarine, at
    room temperature
400g/14oz/2 cups caster sugar
2 eggs, at room temperature
7.5ml/1½ tsp vanilla essence
cocoa powder, for dusting
whipped cream, Greek yogurt or ice
    cream, to serve

1 Preheat the oven to 140°C/275°F/
Gas 1. Sift the flour, salt and
baking powder into a bowl.

2 Place the coffee, brandy, chocolate
and butter or margarine in the top
of a double boiler. Heat until they have
both melted and the mixture is smooth,
stirring occasionally.

3 Pour the chocolate mixture into a
large bowl. Using an electric whisk
on low speed, gradually beat in the
sugar, then whisk until the sugar has
dissolved and the sauce is smooth.

4 Increase the mixer speed to
medium and beat in the sifted flour.
Add the eggs and vanilla essence and
whisk until thoroughly blended.

5 Pour the mixture into a well-
greased 23cm/9in ring mould that
has been lightly dusted with cocoa.
Bake in the oven for about 1 hour 20
minutes, until a skewer inserted in the
cake comes out clean.

6 Leave the cake to cool in the tin for
15 minutes, then turn out on to a
wire rack. Leave to cool completely.

7 When the cake is cold, dust lightly
with cocoa. Serve the cake with
whipped cream, Greek yogurt or ice
cream, as preferred.

BANANA AND LEMON CAKE

Serves 8–10
250g/9oz/2¼ cups plain flour
6.25ml/1¼ tsp baking powder
pinch of salt
115g/4oz/½ cup butter, at room
  temperature
200g/7oz/1 cup caster sugar
90g/3½oz/½ cup soft light
  brown sugar
2 eggs
2.5ml/½ tsp grated lemon rind
225g/8oz/1 cup mashed, very ripe
  bananas
5ml/1 tsp vanilla essence
50ml/2fl oz/¼ cup milk
75g/3oz/¾ cup chopped walnuts

For the icing
115g/4oz/½ cup butter, at room
  temperature
450g/1lb/4½ cups icing sugar
5ml/1 tsp grated lemon rind
45–75ml/3–5 tbsp fresh lemon juice
lemon rind curls, to decorate

1 Preheat the oven to 180°C/350°F/
Gas 4. Grease two 23cm/9in round
cake tins, and line the base of each with
greased greaseproof paper.

2 Sift the flour, baking powder and
salt into a bowl.

3 Beat the butter and sugars in a large
mixing bowl, until light and fluffy.
Beat in the eggs, one at a time, then stir
in the lemon rind.

4 Mix the mashed bananas with the
vanilla and milk in a small bowl.
Stir this, in batches, into the creamed
butter mixture, alternating with the
sifted flour. Stir lightly until just
blended. Fold in the walnuts.

5 Divide the mixture between the
cake tins and spread evenly. Bake
for 30–35 minutes, until a skewer
inserted in the centre comes out clean.
Leave to stand for 5 minutes before
turning out on to a wire rack. Peel off
the greaseproof paper.

6 To make the icing, cream the butter
until smooth, then gradually beat
in the icing sugar. Stir in the lemon rind
and enough of the lemon juice to make
a spreadable consistency.

7 Place one of the cakes on a serving
plate. Spread over one-third of the
icing, then top with the second cake.
Spread the remaining icing evenly over
the top and sides of the cake. Decorate
with lemon rind curls.

FROSTED WALNUT CAKE

Serves 8
225g/8oz/2 cups plain flour
15ml/1 tbsp baking powder
pinch of salt
115g/4oz/¹⁄₂ cup butter or margarine,
*   at room temperature*
200g/7oz/1 cup caster sugar
2 eggs
5ml/1 tsp grated orange rind
5ml/1 tsp vanilla essence
115g/4oz/1 cup finely chopped walnuts
175ml/6fl oz/³⁄₄ cup milk
walnut halves, to decorate

For the icing
115g/4oz/¹⁄₂ cup butter
175g/6oz/³⁄₄ cup soft dark brown sugar
45ml/3 tbsp maple syrup
45ml/3 tbsp milk
200–225g/7–8oz/1³⁄₄–2 cups icing
*   sugar, sifted*

1 Grease two 5cm/2in deep, 20cm/8in cake tins and line the base of each with greased greaseproof paper. Preheat the oven to 190°C/375°F/Gas 5.

2 Sift together the flour, baking powder and salt into a bowl.

VARIATION
To ring the changes, substitute pecan nuts for the walnuts.

3 Beat the butter or margarine to soften, then gradually beat in the caster sugar until light and fluffy. Beat in the eggs, one at a time, then add the grated orange rind and vanilla essence and beat well.

4 Stir in the chopped walnuts, then add the flour and milk in alternate batches, stirring only enough to blend after each addition.

5 Divide the mixture between the prepared cake tins. Bake for about 25 minutes, until a skewer inserted in the centre comes out clean. Cool in the cake tins for 5 minutes before turning out on to a wire rack.

6 To make the icing, melt the butter in a medium-sized saucepan. Add the brown sugar and maple syrup and boil for 2 minutes, stirring constantly.

7 Add the milk to the pan. Bring back to the boil and stir in 25g/1oz/¹⁄₄ cup of the icing sugar. Remove the pan from the heat and leave to cool until lukewarm. Gradually beat in the remaining icing sugar. Set the pan in a bowl of iced water and stir until the icing is thick enough to spread.

8 Spread a little of the icing over one of the cakes. Place the other cake on top. Spread the remaining icing over the top and sides of the cake, then decorate with walnut halves.

FRUIT AND NUT TURNOVERS

————— INGREDIENTS —————

Makes 16
*350g/12oz/2 cups mixed dried fruit,
    such as apricots and prunes*
75g/3oz/¹/₂ cup raisins
115g/4oz/¹/₂ cup soft light brown sugar
*65g/2¹/₂oz/¹/₂ cup pine nuts or chopped
    almonds*
2.5ml/¹/₂ tsp ground cinnamon
oil, for frying
*45ml/3 tbsp caster sugar mixed with
    5ml/1 tsp ground cinnamon, for
    sprinkling*

For the pastry
225g/8oz/2 cups plain flour
1.25ml/¹/₄ tsp baking powder
1.25ml/¹/₄ tsp salt
10ml/2 tsp caster sugar
50g/2oz/4 tbsp unsalted butter, chilled
25g/1oz/2 tbsp white cooking fat
*120–175ml/4–6fl oz/¹/₂–³/₄ cup
    iced water*

1 To make the pastry, sift the flour, baking powder, salt and sugar into a bowl. With a pastry blender or two knives, cut the butter and cooking fat into the flour until the mixture resembles fine breadcrumbs. Sprinkle with 120ml/4fl oz/¹/₂ cup iced water and mix until the dough holds together. If the dough is too crumbly, add a little more water, 15ml/1 tbsp at a time.

2 Gather the dough into a ball and gently flatten into a round. Place in a polythene bag, seal and chill for at least 30 minutes.

3 Place all the dried fruit in a saucepan and add cold water to cover. Bring to the boil, then simmer gently for about 30 minutes, until the fruit is soft enough to purée.

4 Drain the fruit and place in a food processor or blender. Process until smooth, then return the fruit purée to the saucepan. Add the brown sugar and cook for about 5 minutes, stirring constantly, until thick. Remove the pan from the heat and stir in the pine nuts or almonds, and the ground cinnamon. Leave the mixture to cool.

5 Roll out the chilled pastry to 3mm/ ¹/₈in thickness. Stamp out rounds with a 10cm/4in pastry cutter. Re-roll the pastry trimmings and cut out more rounds to make sixteen in all.

COOK'S TIP
The pastry and the filling can both be made up to two days in advance and chilled until needed.

6 Place a spoonful of the fruit in the centre of each pastry round.

7 Moisten the edge of the pastry rounds with water and fold over to form a half-moon shape. Crimp the rounded edge with a fork.

8 Put a 1cm/¹/₂in layer of oil in a heavy frying pan and heat until hot, but not smoking (to test, drop a scrap of pastry into the oil; if the oil sizzles, it is hot enough). Add the turnovers, a few at a time, and fry for about 1¹/₂ minutes on each side, until golden.

9 Drain the turnovers briefly on kitchen paper, then sprinkle with the cinnamon sugar. Serve warm.

SPICY APPLE COOKIES

Makes 36

90g/3¹/₂oz/¹/₂ cup caster sugar
50g/2oz/4 tbsp butter or white cooking
*   fat, at room temperature*
150g/5oz/³/₄ cup thick, ready-made
*   apple sauce*
large pinch of grated lemon rind
115g/4oz/1 cup plain flour
2.5ml/¹/₂ tsp baking powder
1.25ml/¹/₄ tsp bicarbonate of soda
pinch of salt
2.5ml/¹/₂ tsp ground cinnamon
50g/2oz/¹/₂ cup chopped walnuts

COOK'S TIP
If the apple sauce is runny, put it
in a sieve over a bowl and leave to
drain for 10 minutes.

---

1 Preheat the oven to 190°C/375°F/
Gas 5. Beat together the sugar and
butter or cooking fat in a medium-sized
bowl, until light and fluffy and well
blended. Beat in the apple sauce and
grated lemon rind.

2 Sift the flour, baking powder,
baking soda, salt and cinnamon
into the mixture and stir to blend. Add
the chopped walnuts and stir well.

3 Drop teaspoonfuls of the mixture
on to a lightly greased baking sheet,
spacing them about 5cm/2in apart.

4 Bake the biscuits in the centre of
the oven for 8–10 minutes, until
they are golden brown. Transfer the
biscuits to a wire rack to cool.

CHOCOLATE NUT BARS

Makes 32

425g/15oz/2 cups soft light brown
*   sugar*
450g/1lb/2 cups butter or margarine, at
*   room temperature*
2 egg yolks
7.5ml/1¹/₂ tsp vanilla essence
450g/1lb/4 cups wholemeal flour
pinch of salt
225ml/8oz milk chocolate, broken
*   into pieces*
115g/4oz/1 cup chopped walnuts
*   or pecans*

1 Preheat the oven to 180°C/350°F/
Gas 4 and then grease a deep
33 × 23cm/13 × 9in baking tin.

2 Beat together the sugar and butter
or margarine until light and fluffy.
Beat in the egg yolks and vanilla
essence, then stir in the flour and salt.

3 Tip the mixture into the prepared
tin, pressing down with the back of
a spoon. Bake for 25–30 minutes, until
lightly browned.

4 Remove the tin from the oven and
immediately place the chocolate
pieces on the hot biscuit base. Leave
until the chocolate softens, then spread
evenly with a palette knife. Sprinkle
with the nuts, and while warm, cut into
bars. Cool before serving.

LOUISIANA CINNAMON CRISPS

Makes about 20
225g/8oz/2 cups plain flour
pinch of salt
15ml/1 tbsp baking powder
5ml/1 tsp ground cinnamon
2 eggs
40g/1½oz/¼ cup caster sugar
175ml/6fl oz/¾ cup milk
2.5ml/½ tsp vanilla essence
oil, for deep-frying
icing sugar, for sprinkling

1 To make the dough, sift together the flour, salt, baking powder and ground cinnamon into a medium-sized mixing bowl.

2 In a separate bowl, whisk the eggs, caster sugar, milk and vanilla essence. Pour the egg mixture into the dry ingredients and mix together quickly to form a soft dough.

3 Turn out the dough on to a lightly floured surface and knead until smooth and elastic.

4 Heat the oil in a deep-fryer or a large, heavy-based saucepan to 190°C/375°F. Roll out the dough on a floured surface to a 5mm/¼in thick round. Slice diagonally into diamonds, about 7.5cm/3in long.

5 Fry the crisps in the hot oil, turning once, until golden brown on both sides. Remove with tongs or a slotted spoon and drain well on kitchen paper. Sprinkle the crisps generously with sifted icing sugar before serving.

SPICY ANISEED BISCUITS

INGREDIENTS

Makes 24

175g/6oz/1½ cups plain flour
5ml/1 tsp baking powder
pinch of salt
115g/4oz/½ cup unsalted butter, at
   room temperature
90g/3½oz/½ cup caster sugar
1 egg
5ml/1 tsp aniseed
15ml/1 tbsp brandy
40g/1½oz/¼ cup caster sugar mixed
   with 2.5ml/½ tsp ground cinnamon,
   for sprinkling

1 Sift together the flour, baking powder and salt into a bowl.

2 Beat the butter with the sugar until light and fluffy, then beat in the egg, aniseed and brandy. Add the sifted flour mixture and stir to make a soft dough. Knead lightly, then wrap in clear film and chill for 30 minutes.

3 Preheat the oven to 180°C/350°F/ Gas 4. Grease two baking sheets.

4 Roll out the chilled dough on a lightly floured surface to about 3mm/⅛in thickness.

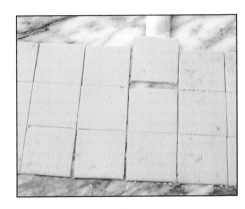

5 With a cutter, pastry wheel, or knife, cut out the biscuits into squares, diamonds, rounds or any shape you prefer. Re-roll trimmings in order to use up all the dough.

6 Place the biscuits on the prepared baking sheets and sprinkle lightly with the cinnamon sugar.

7 Bake for about 10 minutes, until just golden. Cool on the baking sheet for 5 minutes before transferring to a wire rack to cool completely. The biscuits can be kept in an airtight container for up to one week.

HOT WHITE CHOCOLATE

INGREDIENTS

Serves 4
175g/6oz white chocolate
1.75 litres/3 pints/7½ cups milk
5ml/1 tsp coffee extract, or 10ml/2 tsp
instant coffee powder
10ml/2 tsp orange-flavoured
liqueur (optional)
whipped cream and ground cinnamon,
to serve

> **COOK'S TIP**
> Use milk chocolate or plain
> chocolate instead of white
> chocolate if you prefer, but taste
> before serving – you may wish to
> add a little sugar.

1 Finely chop the white chocolate with a sharp knife. (Try not to handle it too much or it will soften and stick together.)

2 Pour the milk into a large heavy-based saucepan and heat until almost boiling and bubbles form around the edge of the pan.

3 Add the chopped white chocolate, coffee extract or powder, and orange-flavoured liqueur if using. Stir until the chocolate has melted.

4 Pour the hot chocolate into four mugs. Top each with a swirl or spoonful of whipped cream and a sprinkling of ground cinnamon. Serve immediately.

EASY CHOCOLATE HAZELNUT FUDGE

INGREDIENTS

Makes 16 squares
150ml/¼ pint/⅔ cup evaporated
milk
350g/12oz/1¾ cups sugar
large pinch of salt
50g/2oz/½ cup hazelnuts, halved
350g/12oz/2 cups plain chocolate chips

1 Generously grease a 20cm/8in square cake tin.

> **VARIATION**
> For Easy Peanut Fudge, replace
> the halved hazelnuts with
> chopped, unsalted peanuts.

2 Place the evaporated milk, sugar and salt in a heavy-based saucepan. Bring to the boil over a medium heat, stirring constantly. Simmer gently, stirring, for about 5 minutes.

3 Remove the pan from the heat and add the hazelnuts and chocolate chips. Stir gently until the chocolate has completely melted.

4 Quickly pour the fudge mixture into the prepared tin and spread evenly. Leave to cool and set.

5 When the fudge has set, cut it into 2.5cm/1in squares. Store in an airtight container, separating the layers with greaseproof paper.

INDEX